Physical Characteristics of the Weimaraner

(from The Kennel Club breed standard)

Hindquarters: Moderately angulated, with well turned stifle. Hocks well let down, turned neither in nor out. Musculation well developed.

Tail: Customarily docked so that remaining tail covers scrotum in dogs and vulva in bitches. Thickness of tail in proportion to body, and should be carried in a manner expressing confidence and sound temperament. In Long-haired, tip of tail may be removed.

Colour: Preferably silver grey, shades of mouse or roe grey permissible, blending to lighter shade on head and ears. Dark eel stripe frequently occurs along back. Whole coat gives appearance of metallic sheen. Small white marks permissible on chest. White spots resulting from injuries not penalised.

Body: Length of body from highest point of withers to root of tail should equal the measurement from the highest point of withers to ground. Topline level, with slightly sloping croup. Chest well developed, deep. Shoulders well laid. Ribs well sprung, ribcage extending well back. Abdomen firmly held, moderately tucked-up flank. Brisket should drop to elbow.

Feet: Firm, compact. Toes well arched, pads close, thick. Nails short, grey or amber in colour. Dew claws customarily removed.

Size: Height at withers: dogs: 61-69 cms (25–27 ins); bitches: 56-64 cms (22–25 ins).

Weimaraner

by Lavonia Harper

Table of Contents

PUBLISHED IN THE
UNITED KINGDOM BY:

INTERPET
PUBLISHING

Vincent Lane, Dorking
Surrey RH4 3YX
England

ISBN 1-902389-09-3

74
Housebreaking and Training Your Weimaraner

by Charlotte Schwartz
Be informed about the importance of training your Weimaraner from the basics of housebreaking and understanding the development of a young dog to executing obedience commands (sit, stay, down, etc.).

Photos by Carol Ann Johnson

with additional photos by:
Norvia Behling
TJ Calhoun
Carolina Biological Supply
Doskocil
Isabelle Francais
James Hayden-Yoav
James R Hayden, RBP
Bill Jonas
Alice van Kempen

Dwight R Kuhn
Dr Dennis Kunkel
Charles & Mary McGee
Mikki Pet Products
Phototake
Jean Claude Revy
Dr Andrew Spielman
Karen Taylor
C James Webb

Illustrations by Renée Low

132
Your Senior Weimaraner

Recognise the signs of an ageing dog, both behavioural and medical; implement a senior-care programme with your veterinary surgeon and become comfortable with making the final decisions and arrangements for your senior Weimaraner.

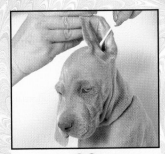

99
Health Care of Your Weimaraner

Discover how to select a proper veterinary surgeon and care for your dog at all stages of life. Topics include vaccination scheduling, skin problems, dealing with parasites and the medical conditions common to the breed, including a section on eye problems.

140
Showing Your Weimaraner

Experience the dog show world, including different types of shows and the making up of a champion. Go beyond the conformation ring to working trials and agility trials, etc.

The 'grey ghost,' as the Weimaraner has been named, has captured the imaginations of writers, hunters and dog lovers for generations.

HISTORY OF THE
WEIMARANER

A grey spectre poised on a misty meadow, forepaw raised; an illusion of molten silver blending into the fog. Two golden eyes pierce the smoky haze. Vision, artform or ancient canid? For centuries, the 'grey ghost' called the Weimaraner has captivated the souls and imaginations of hunters, artists and dog aficionados.

Cloaked in mystery and controversy, the Weimaraner remains as much a paradox today as it was centuries ago when it was closely guarded by German royalty, who prized the dog's power and endurance. Revered also for his loyalty and devotion to his master, the Weimaraner was sometimes called upon to defend his hunter/master from the wildebeest encountered during the hunt. Although it has evolved into a prized family hunting companion, the Weimaraner's original instincts remain strong. Highly intelligent and affectionate, it is fearless and protective and will still track and retrieve wildfowl as well as furred game such as fox or rabbit.

Weimaraner

In keeping with its ghostly image, the Weimaraner's history is blurred by speculation. In a 1972 publication, Klaus Hartmann (Weimaraner breeding regulator from 1963 until 1975) presented his conclusion that the Weimaraner can be traced back to the grey Leithunde (leash/lead dogs) of the Royal French Hirschmeuten (red deer packs) in the 1600s. Such theories are supported by examinations of wood carvings and art work from the Middle Ages.

Dogs resembling the modern Weimaraner have been depicted in sculptures, tapestries and paintings as early as the 12th century. Some Medieval art depicts Weimaraner-type dogs surrounding a captured unicorn. The dogs are of solid colour, many of grey hue, and have powerful stocky bodies, long backs and heavy heads, with moderately long ears and draping upper lips. A Van Dyck painting from 1631 shows a Weimaraner look-alike seated beside Prince Rupprecht von Pfalz.

The Bruno de Jura is a modern-day Swiss scent hound who shares common ancestors with the Weimaraner in the St. Hubertus Brachen.

The Bloodhound is the direct descendant of the St. Hubert hounds of years gone by. As such, the Bloodhound derives from similar bloodlines as today's Weimaraner.

In another comprehensive study of the breed, breed expert Ludwig Beckmann writes of dogs that are dark grey, with a few of silver grey. Ears are long, narrow and twisted, and the head is narrow when viewed from the front. He describes the dogs as being very devoted to their masters. 'They can readily distinguish their master's voice and horn. No encouragement is needed during the hunt where they are equally energetic in hot or cold weather.'

The most accepted theories allow that today's Weimaraner descended from the St. Hubertus Brachen, a powerful hunting hound named for the monks who resided at the Benedictine Cloistered Monastery of St. Hubert in the Ardennes mountains. These long-bodied dogs were black, with red or fawn-coloured markings over their eyes and on their legs, with an occasional small white patch on the chest. Although such markings are unacceptable under today's Weimaraner breed standard, Weimaraner pups are still sometimes born bearing ginger-coloured spots over the eyes and on the legs.

The first known pure-bred Weimaraners were developed by the Grand Duke Karl August during the late 1700s. The Grand Duke resided in Weimar, Germany, his estate surrounded by dense forests thick with wild game such as stag, boar, bear and wolves. An avid sportsman who hunted a variety of big game, he discovered the powerful grey dog while

DID YOU KNOW?

Weimaraners have been known to follow scents that baffled Bloodhounds. During the US

White Sands missile testing project, the government used Weimaraners to detect and recover pieces of spent projectiles that human searchers failed to find.

pleasure. As a powerful aristocrat, he was able to dictate who would be permitted to own or hunt with the exceptional dogs he bred. His breeding stock and offspring were stringently protected, and only selected family members or privileged nobility were allowed to own his dogs. None were permitted to become simply pets or family companions.

The Duke's protective attitude surrounding the Weimaraner was adopted by anyone who owned his dogs, and it persisted into the late 1800s. The breed was still virtually unknown to the German public at the beginning of the 20th century.

In 1897, the Weimaraner Club of Germany was formed with the express purpose of protecting and improving the breed under very strict guidelines. Membership was restricted; promoting the breed was not a Club objective, and only members were permitted to own or breed the dogs. Club members took great pains to prevent a Weimaraner from going to anyone who might exploit the breed. They simply believed that the average sportsman was not capable of appreciating the superior qualities of their favoured breed. In their quest to retain only the very best animals as breeding

hunting on the estate of Bohemian Prince Esterhazy e Aversperg. He became enamoured with the dog's enormous strength, courage and endurance, and felt that these attributes would be valuable assets to his hunting challenges.

The Duke decided to develop this dog for his personal hunting

stock, the Club limited to 1500 the total number of dogs allowed to be registered with the Club.

Type and temperament were carefully moulded. As the large game population declined during the latter half of the 19th century, the Weimaraner was refined from a deer and bear hunter to a fur and feathers dog. His ancient instincts remain strong, however, and must be an important factor for anyone who considers buying a Weimaraner.

In 1935 the Weimaraner Club of Germany and the Austrian Weimaraner Club (founded in 1924) drew up and completed the official breed standard for the Weimaraner. The famous Austrian author Ludwig von Merey von Kapos Mere, an influential authority on hunting dogs, is credited for joining Otto Stockmeyer, head of the Austrian Weimaraner Club, and Major Robert A D Herber, president of the German Weimaraner Club, in their collaborative effort to complete the standard. Major Herber bred Weimaraners under the Wulssriede affix. His devotion to his chosen breed was so renowned that he was fondly referred to as the 'Father of the Weimaraner.'

The Weimaraner's strength and popularity in its native Germany must be attributed in part to the widely respected

Information...

Weimaraner puppies are born with eyes of a bright sapphire blue which begins to fade at

about 6 weeks of age. The yellow-orange pigment first appears as spikes of colour, slowly merging into a more uniform shade. Some Weimaraners mature with eyes of two different hues.

Weimaraner breeder Heinz Reuper (1923–1995), German sportsman and renowned field trial judge. During his 40 years in the breed, Reuper bred 30 litters under his vom Zenthof affix, and was staunch in training all of his Weimaraners to their Meister Prufung (Master Hunting Certificate). His field trial bitch, Otti vom Elchwinkel, became the top-winning hunting Weimaraner of all time and was famous among field trial judges for her superb scenting ability. In his youth Reuper hunted over his dogs without using a shotgun, as guns were illegal in Germany after World War II. True to their ancient instincts, Reuper's Weimaraners tracked

fox and other furred animals, and killed them at the throat.

DEVELOPMENT AND RECOGNITION IN THE UNITED STATES

The next phase of Weimaraner history occurred in the United States in 1928. New England sportsman Howard Knight became enamoured with the breed through his German friend, Fritz Grossman. Knight imported a Weimaraner dog and bitch who later turned up sterile. As a show of good intent, Knight kept the dogs and worked them regularly in the field, which further advanced his admiration for this powerful hunting dog. In 1929, with Grossman's support, he became the first American citizen to be accepted into the Weimaraner Club of Germany. Finally, in 1938, Major Herber of the German Club sent Knight four Weimaraners; two litter sisters, Dorle and Adda v Schwarzen Kamp; a year-old bitch, Aura v Gailberg; and a puppy dog, Mars aus der Wulfsreide. Aura became the first Weimaraner to earn an obedience Companion Dog title, and her son, Ch Grafmar's Jupiter UTD, was the first to complete all the obedience degrees. During the next 10 years, 36 Grafmar Weimaraners earned titles in obedience.

The breed was recognised by the American Kennel Club in 1942, and the Weimaraner Club of America was founded the following year, with Knight at the helm as the first president.

Weimaraners first entered US field trials in 1948. As the breed continued to grow in popularity during the post-war years, the German Club became concerned with quality and standards and decided to limit foreign sales.

AKC registrations peaked in 1957 with over 10,000 Weimaraners registered. Not surprisingly, novice breeding proliferated and breed quality suffered. Too many Weimaraners were poorly bred, bad-tempered and ugly, and both good and poor pups ended up in the wrong hands, with people who were ill-equipped to live with a large, highly intelligent and energetic hunting dog. Not surprisingly, popularity declined over the next three decades, and by the late 1980s, registrations numbered a more acceptable three to four thousand. However, it remains true today that buyers need to educate themselves about Weimaraner temperament and needs before purchasing a pup.

WEIMARANERS IN THE UNITED KINGDOM

Two decades after Howard Knight embraced the Weimaraner, two British Army officers stationed in Germany took notice of Weimaraners owned by American Air Force personnel stationed in the American Zone. Major R H Petty and Lt Col. Eric Richardson negotiated with a German contact to acquire their first Weimaraners. Ultimately Major Petty imported a bitch, Cobra von Boberstrand, and a dog, Bando von Fohr, to England in 1952, the first Weimaraners on record to be introduced to the UK. Petty later acquired six more and registered the three most promising with the Kennel Club.

Lt Col. Richardson imported five Weimaraners, but registered only two with The Kennel Club. A third fancier, Mrs Olga Mallet, also imported a dog and a bitch. These nine Weimaraners

This lovely Weimaraner was bred in Holland, where the breed has many admirers.

Weimaraner

Information...

In 1996 there were 18 International Weimaraner Clubs in 14 different countries. Four of those clubs are in Australia.

Great Britain was founded in 1953, Major Petty served as its first secretary.

THE LONGHAIRED WEIMARANER

Although the longhaired Weimaraner receives less attention due to the prominence of its shorthaired relative, a strong camp of Longhair admirers are still devoted to this elegant variety of the breed. Like the shorthaired Weimaraner, the Longhair is a versatile and tractable hunting partner, the difference being primarily in coat.

The coat of a Longhair whelp is soft and woolly, compared to the crisp coat of the shorthaired pup. The mature Longhair coat is straight or slightly wavy, with a silky texture, tight on the upper body and less so on the lower part. The outer ears are covered with long, soft, silky hair, and the tail is heavily feathered and plume-like, with more soft feathering on the backs of the legs and between the toes. The tail is not docked, as is that of the shorthaired Weimaraner.

Coat length can range between long and the original coarse shorter hair, and should be smooth and thick, resistant to weather and thorns, with a water-repellent undercoat. In Germany, the shorthaired variety

registered with The Kennel Club became the foundation stock for the breed in the UK. Lt Col. Richardson bred under the Monksway affix. Mrs Mallet adopted the affix Ipley, but bred only two litters before returning to her native Canada.

Major Petty and his wife bred their Weimaraners under the Strawbridge affix, producing Ch Strawbridge Oliver, the first UK champion in the breed. When the Weimaraner Club of

The Longhaired Weimaraner possesses a straight or slightly wavy coat of silky hair. In Germany, the Longhaired variety was used on waterfowl due to its protective coat.

was used mostly for upland game birds, and the longhaired dogs were used primarily for waterfowl because of their dense, protective undercoat.

The Longhair gene is recessive, with the Shorthair being dominant. Longhaired puppies can occur if both shorthaired parents carry the Longhair gene, but Longhair bred to Longhair will always produce longhaired pups.

Weimaraner breedings will sometimes produce a shorter, coarser coat type called the Stockhaarig, which is a mixture between Longhair and Shorthair types. When such situations occur, the registration number is followed by an (LK) designation, indicating long/short coat. Longhair breeders occasionally breed to LK to improve the quality and resilience of the long coat; they must receive special permission in order to do so. It is noteworthy that a Longhair, Aruni Dinwiddi from Seicer, bred by Ann Jansen, is recorded as the first Weimaraner to win a Challenge Certificate in Britain.

17

Today's Weimaraner still possesses many of the traits that made him a legend during ancient hunting times. He has great endurance, with a special passion for both tracking and scenting. In the field he is not a 'big running' dog, and some modern theorists contend this is because he likes his owner so much that he prefers to stay nearby. That may be

The colour of the Weimaraner is preferably silver grey, but mouse grey or similar shades are permissible under the standard.

accurate, as Weimaraners are extremely loyal and can be protective of their masters, families and property, but such watchdog instincts should not be nurtured or encouraged. They are also bold and assertive, headstrong and very energetic, qualities that may make them unsuitable for inexperienced dog owners. Because the Weimaraner was developed as a hunter of both small game and fowl, he may be dangerous to birds and small mammals such as cats or small dogs.

Like most other large hunting breeds, the Weimaraner needs a lot of exercise and must be controlled to prevent him from ranging in search of game. This is a very energetic animal who was bred to hunt all day with his master. Anyone who is unable to deal with this behaviour should consider another breed that is less animated.

The Weimaraner's rambunctious nature requires consistent obedience training, ideally as early as possible, to control his exuberant behaviour. Puppy classes and control exercises are essential to teach him that he must respect and obey all

Weimaraners are considered 'easy keepers' and can easily be groomed at home. Their smooth coat will retain its sheen with weekly polishing with a bristle brush or a hound mitt, although more frequent grooming is good for human bonding as well as coat maintenance, especially for the Longhair. A chamois leather is good for stimulating circulation as well as for drying the coat after a bath.

Despite the myth and folklore surrounding the Weimaraner, he is not a pariah or a wonder dog. He can and will be as good or as difficult as opportunity allows.

The Weimaraner is an active dog, eager to learn, and always ready for direction and praise for a job well done.

members of the family. Training methods must be firm but gentle, as the Weimaraner is as sensitive as he is energetic, and harsh treatment will crush his attitude and spirit.

Most Weimaraners will bark to alert their owners at the approach of strangers or anything they perceive as threatening. If they are left alone for long periods of time, they may bark incessantly and could become destructive or develop undesirable habits. Even though a hunting dog, this breed is very much a 'people dog' and requires your attention and affection. He is basically a housedog and will not thrive if he is confined to a kennel or outside area. Whether hunting or at home, he needs security in his relation-ship with his master.

WEIMARANER ACTIVITIES
In the United States and most European countries, every hunting breed performs a special task. Pointing dogs must seek and point before the game is flushed, and be steady to the shot. Retrievers flush the birds and retrieve them after they are shot. In heavily wooded areas, spaniels drive the birds. Waterfowl hunting requires breeds with coats that make them suitable for water work. Hounds are used to follow the blood track of the wounded deer, and some smaller breeds are used for hunting fox.

The Weimaraner belongs to the gundog group called HPR breeds—'jack-of-all-trades' gundogs that do it all...*hunt, point and retrieve.* HPR breeds include

19

the Brittany, German Shorthaired Pointer (GSP), German Wirehaired Pointer (GWP), Hungarian Vizsla, Italian Spinone, Large Munster-lander and, of course, the Weimaraner.

GERMAN AND AUSTRIAN FIELD WORK While the typical field trial is designed to test for specific breed abilities, it is understandably difficult to test a tri-purpose HPR dog like the Weimaraner. In Germany and Austria, where the Weimaraner is still revered for his versatility, there are specialised field trials in which the HPR breeds must perform all the tasks for which they were originally bred.

The Weimaraner excels on the field and enjoys the opportunity to accompany its owner on hunting expeditions.

For a given year, a young Weimaraner who had been born either in the previous year or during the last three months of the year before that, must first pass the *Verbands-Jugendprufung* (VJP) in the spring. This is a Youth Test where the dog will have to search, point, work out the track of a hare and show he is not afraid of the shot. In the autumn of the same year, he enters the *Herbst Zuchtprufung* (HZP). In this test, the dog must prove his hunting ability. He will search and point, as well as retrieve game (pheasant) and track a dragged pheasant. He also faces water work, such as searching the reeds for a lost duck and retrieving it from water. In Germany you are allowed to breed your Weimaraner only if he has passed his HZP.

The *Vollgebrauchsprufung* (VGP) in Austria and the *Verbands-Gebrauchsprufung* (VGP) in Germany represent the highest test for experienced, well-trained HPRs. The test takes two days and demands hard work of both dog and handler. The German VGP contains at least 28 subjects or tasks that are judged separately. In the German states where work on live ducks is allowed, this 29th test is added.

The VGP is divided into five groups with complex situations contrived in each of those groups. The dogs are judged on many

If properly socialised, Weimaraners are accepting of other house pets, such as the family cat. Acquiring a puppy and a kitten simultaneously encourages the ideal rapport between housemates.

different levels and categories of each ability (searching, pointing and retrieving). Additionally, the dog and handler are evaluated on how they work together as a team, and the dog is evaluated on his endurance, the way he hunts and his willingness to please. The system of points and prizes awarded is complicated and most difficult to understand. On the German or Austrian pedigree, the points and prize designation will appear behind the dog's name, i.e. VGP II 254, which means a second prize with 254 points. The Austrian VGP has 35 subjects, thus a higher score may appear on that pedigree.

The VGP is one of the most demanding tests of the HPR and the demands on both dog and handler over the two-day period are extremely difficult. Neither

dog nor handler can be insufficient on any of the subjects that are required for a passing grade.

Judging of the spring VJP and the autumn HZP is more forgiving, as the judge will allow for the inexperience of the team. However, at the VGP both dog and

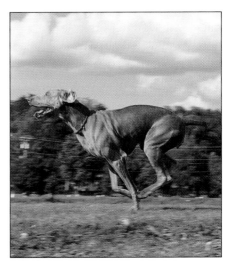

With training and conditioning, the Weimaraner can compete in a variety of dog sports, able to pass the most rigorous field tests.

handler are expected to arrive very well prepared and little quarter is given for weaknesses or errors. A new German rule permits a second attempt at the VGP if you fail the first attempt, but none beyond that. This rule prevents people from making a sport of the VGP by entering several just to get the highest test results in points.

Another rule in Germany and Austria declares that only hunters may enter the VGP, whereas in England and other European countries, people who do not hunt with their dogs themselves are allowed to participate. The German restriction is intended to preserve the test for working dogs that are actually used for hunting.

The Weimaraner is a healthy, active dog. Acquire a properly bred dog, whose parents are tested for eye and hip diseases, to ensure a long-lived companion for you.

HUNTING AND ROUGH SHOOTING

Although most Weimaraners have the instinct to hunt, point and retrieve depending on their individual ancestry, every Weimaraner will still benefit from some degree of training. A wise owner bent on hunting with his dog should align himself with an experienced hunter or competitor in order to train his dog correctly. Training is best begun at an early age before the pup acquires bad habits that could interfere with his willingness to work in tandem with his master.

HEALTH CONCERNS

Unlike many breeds who have suffered serious health problems due to surges in popularity, the Weimaraner is a relatively healthy breed that requires basic common-sense care to maintain good health and spirit in the dog.

HIP DYSPLASIA (HD)

Hip dysplasia simply means poor or abnormal development of the hip joint where the ball and socket do not function properly. It is common in most large breeds of dogs and is considered to be an inherited disorder. To diagnose HD, your veterinarian will x-ray your dog and submit those films to the British Veterinary Association and The Kennel Club for evaluation. A severe case of HD can render a working dog worthless in the field or other

DO YOU KNOW ABOUT HIP DYSPLASIA?

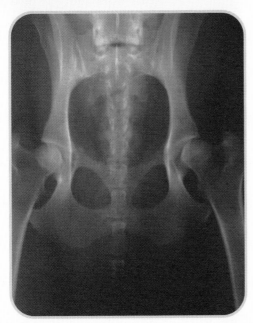

X-ray of a dog with 'Good' hips.

X-ray of a dog with 'Moderate' dysplastic hips.

Hip dysplasia is a fairly common condition found in purebred dogs. When a dog has hip dysplasia, its hind leg has an incorrectly formed hip joint. By constant use of the hip joint, it becomes more and more loose, wears abnormally and may become arthritic.

Hip dysplasia can only be confirmed with an x-ray, but certain symptoms may indicate a problem. Your dog may have a hip dysplasia problem if it walks in a peculiar manner, hops instead of smoothly runs, uses his hind legs in unison (to keep the pressure off the weak joint), has trouble getting up from a prone position or always sits with both legs together on one side of its body.

As the dog matures, it may adapt well to life with a bad hip, but in a few years the arthritis develops and many dogs with hip dysplasia become cripples.

Hip dysplasia is considered an inherited disease and only can be diagnosed definitively when the dog is two years old. Some experts claim that a special diet might help your puppy outgrow the bad hip, but the usual treatments are surgical. The removal of the pectineus muscle, the removal of the round part of the femur, reconstructing the pelvis and replacing the hip with an artificial one are all surgical interventions that are expensive, but they are usually very successful. Follow the advice of your veterinary surgeon.

Overfeeding as well as genetic factors play an important role in the appearance of hip dysplasia in Weimaraners. The larger the dog, the more prone it is to having a hip or elbow problem.

ation has joined with The Kennel Club to help curb the incidence of hip dysplasia in all breeds of dogs. Weimaraners over one year of age and under six years of age should be x-rayed by a veterinary surgeon. The x-rays are submitted to a special board of veterinarians who specialise in reading orthopaedic films. If the dog shows no evidence of abnormality, The Kennel Club issues a certificate of clearance. To correctly identify the dog under evaluation, The Kennel Club requires the dog's date of birth and Kennel Club registration number to be recorded on the

activities, and even a mild case can cause painful arthritis in the average house dog.

While hip dysplasia is a largely inherited condition, research shows that environmental factors play a significant role in its development. Overfeeding and feeding a diet high in calories (primarily fat) during a large-breed puppy's rapid-growth stages are suspected to be contributing factors in the development of HD. Heavy-bodied and overweight puppies are more at risk than pups with very lean conformation.

The British Veterinary Associ-

HOW TO PREVENT BLOAT

Research has confirmed that the structure of the Weimaraner contributes to his predisposition to this condition. Nevertheless, there are several precautions you can take to reduce the risk.
• Feed your dog twice daily rather than offer one large meal.
• Do not exercise your dog for at least an hour before and two hours after eating.
• Make sure your dog is calm and not overly excited while he's eating. It has been shown that nervous or overly excited dogs are more prone to develop bloat.
• Add a small portion of moist meat product to his dried food ration.

x-ray. The purpose of such screening is to eliminate affected dogs from breeding programmes, with the long-term goal of reducing the incidence of HD in the affected breeds.

Weimaraners who show marked evidence of hip dysplasia should never be bred. Anyone looking for a healthy Weimaraner pup should make certain the sire and dam of any litter under consideration have their certificates of clearance.

BLOAT (GASTRIC DILATION/ VOLVULUS)

Bloat is a life-threatening condition that is most common in very deep-chested breeds such as the Weimaraner, Irish Setter, Bloodhound, Great Dane and several other similarly constructed breeds. It occurs when the stomach fills up rapidly with air and begins to twist, cutting off the blood supply. If not treated immediately, the dog will go into shock and die.

The development of bloat is sudden and unexplainable. The dog will become restless and his stomach will appear swollen or distended, and he will have difficulty breathing. The dog must receive veterinary attention at once in order to survive. The vet must relieve the pressure in the stomach and surgically return the stomach to its normal position.

ENTROPION

Entropion causes the eyelids to roll in, causing the eyelashes to rub on the cornea, creating great discomfort. Eventual scarring may cause some vision loss. The condition can be surgically corrected, but affected dogs should not be bred.

You can avoid bloat, hip dysplasia and obesity by following simple feeding rules. Limit your Weimaraner's activity before and after meals. Do not overfeed your Weimaraner and keep adolescents lean.

25

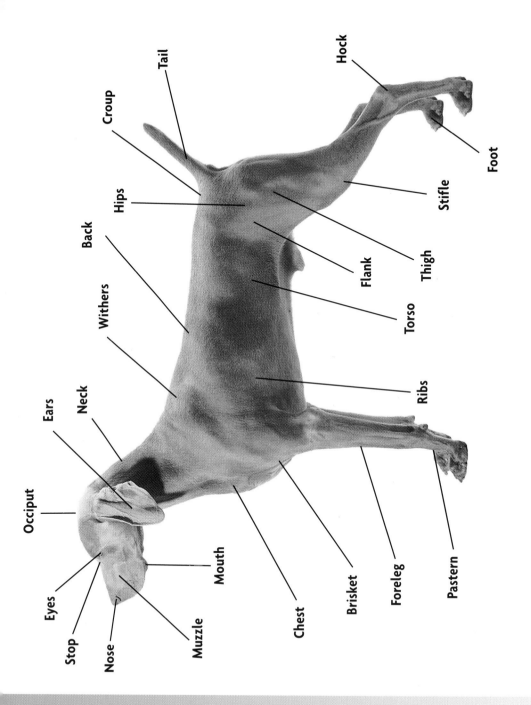

Tail

Croup

Hock

Foot

Stifle

Hips

Thigh

Back

Flank

Withers

Torso

Neck

Ears

Ribs

Occiput

Eyes

Stop

Nose

Muzzle

Mouth

Chest

Brisket

Foreleg

Pastern

Physical Structure of the Weimaraner

BREED STANDARD FOR THE
WEIMARANER

The British, American and German breed standards for the Weimaraner are basically very similar, although the British version is less specific and therefore subject to more individual interpretation. Although all three standards stress working ability, the German standard is much more explicit and includes a section on behaviour and character. It is repeated here to illustrate the German emphasis on working skills and temperament:

'A versatile, easy-going, fearless and enthusiastic gundog with a systematic and persevering search, yet not excessively fast. A remarkably good nose. Sharp on prey and game. Also man-sharp, yet not aggressive. Reliable in pointing and waterwork. Remarkable inclination to the work after the shot.'

The German standard is also more specific on the physical properties of the Weimaraner and covers many more individual body parts, including even the

The Weimaraner's gait (or movement) should be effortless and ground covering, according to the standard. Handlers must demonstrate their dogs' gait for the judge so he can evaluate the dog's movement and structure.

skin of the dog. The section on size also includes correct weight, unmentioned in either the British or American standard. The German section on faults is also more detailed, assigning 16 specific areas to be faulted and further listing 16 disqualifying faults.

The breed standard should be studied and thoroughly understood by anyone considering a Weimaraner as a hunting or family companion. The Weimaraner makes a wonderful working dog, pet or show dog as long as one is aware of the dog's temperament and instincts and is adequately prepared to deal with them in a manner best suited to the dog.

THE KENNEL CLUB BREED STANDARD FOR THE WEIMARANER

General Appearance: Medium size, grey with light eyes. Presents a picture of power, stamina and balance.

The ears are correct.

The ears are too short.

Weimaraners should be exhibited in top condition, which is achieved through proper feeding, exercise and grooming.

The Weimaraner's head should be aristocatic and moderately long.

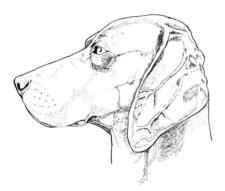

A nice profile view, showing a fine head.

A correct head.

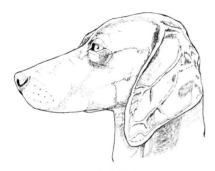

An undesirable head,
showing a weak muzzle and lack of flews.

Eyes: Medium-sized, round. Shades of amber or blue-grey. Placed far enough apart to indicate good disposition, not too protruding or deeply set. Expression keen, kind and intelligent.

Ears: Long, lobular, slightly folded, set high. When drawn alongside the jaw, should end approximately 2.5 cms (1 in) from point of nose.

Characteristics: Hunting ability of paramount concern.

Head and Skull: Moderately long, aristocratic; moderate stop, slight median line extending back over forehead. Rather prominent occipital bone. Measurement from top of nose to stop equal to measurement from stop to occipital prominence. Flews moderately deep, enclosing powerful jaw. Foreface straight and delicate at the nostrils. Skin tightly drawn. Nose grey.

The chest of the Weimaraner should be well developed and deep.

Weimaraner

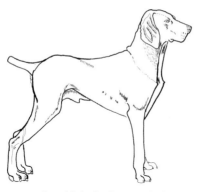

An undesirable body, showing a high rear and too much tuck up.

An undesirable body, showing an under-developed chest.

Body: Length of body from highest point of withers to root of tail should equal the measurement from the highest point of withers to ground. Topline level, with slightly sloping croup. Chest well developed, deep. Shoulders well laid. Ribs well sprung, ribcage extending well back. Abdomen firmly held, moderately tucked-up flank. Brisket should drop to elbow.

Hindquarters: Moderately angulated, with well turned stifle. Hocks well let down, turned neither in nor out. Musculation well developed.

Feet: Firm, compact. Toes well arched, pads close, thick. Nails short, grey or amber in colour. Dew claws customarily removed.

The Weimaraner's bite is checked during conformational judging.

Mouth: Jaws strong with a perfect, regular and complete scissor bite, i.e. upper teeth closely overlapping lower teeth and set square to the jaws. Lips and gums of pinkish, flesh colour. Complete dentition highly desirable.

Neck: Clean-cut and moderately long.

Forequarters: Forelegs straight and strong. Measurement from elbow to ground equal to distance from elbow to top of withers.

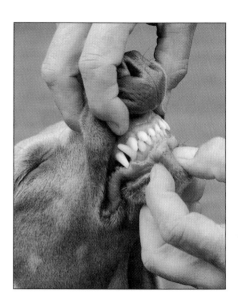

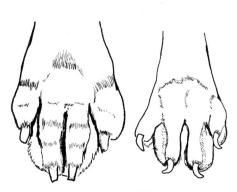

Left: A correct front foot. Right: A splay foot, showing nails that are too long.

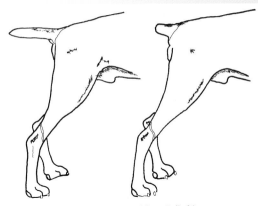

The correct tail length (left); tail too short (right).

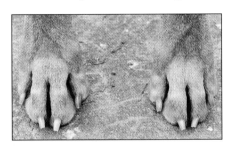

Tail: Customarily docked so that remaining tail covers scrotum in dogs and vulva in bitches. Thickness of tail in proportion to body, and should be carried in a manner expressing confidence and sound temperament. In Longhaired, tip of tail may be removed.

Proper Weimaraner front feet, showing nails of the correct length.

The Longhaired Weimaraner is identical to its shorthaired counterpart in every way except coat, which is longer on body, neck, chest, belly, tail and limbs.

The profile of a shorthaired dog compared to that of a Longhaired Weimaraner.

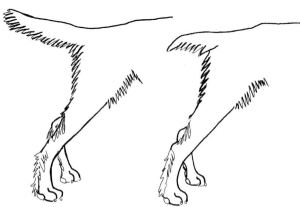

The Longhaired variety posses a full-length tail, possibly with tip removed.

Gait/Movement: Effortless, ground covering, indicating smooth co-ordination. Seen from rear, hind feet parallel to front feet. Seen from side, topline remains strong and level.

Coat: Short, smooth and sleek. In Long-haired variety, coat from 2.5–5 cms (1–2 ins) long on body, somewhat longer on neck, chest and belly. Tail and back of limbs, feathered.

Colour: Preferably silver grey, shades of mouse or roe grey permissible, blending to lighter shade on head and ears. Dark eel stripe frequently occurs along back. Whole coat gives appearance of metallic sheen. Small white marks permissible on chest. White spots resulting from injuries not penalised.

Size: Height at withers: dogs: 61-69 cms (25–27 ins); bitches: 56-64 cms (22–25 ins).

Faults: Any departure from the foregoing points should be considered a fault and the seriousness with which the fault should be regarded should be in exact proportion to its degree.

Note: Male animals should have two apparently normal testicles fully descended into the scrotum.

WEIMARANER

WHERE TO BEGIN?

To locate a quality Weimaraner, it is easier to first find a quality breeder. Locating a litter of Weimaraners should not present a problem for the new owner. You should enquire about breeders in your area who enjoy a good reputation in the breed. You are looking for an established breeder with outstanding dog ethics and a strong commitment to the breed. New owners should have as many questions as they have doubts. An established breeder is indeed the one to answer your four million questions and make you comfortable with your choice of the Weimaraner. An established breeder will sell you a puppy at a fair price if, and only if, the breeder determines that you are a suitable, worthy owner of his/her dogs. An established breeder can be relied upon for advice, no matter what time of day or night. A reputable breeder will accept a puppy back, without questions, should you decide that this is not the right dog for you.

When choosing a breeder,

DID YOU KNOW?

Unfortunately, when a puppy is bought by someone who does not take into consideration the time and attention that dog ownership requires, it is the puppy who suffers when he is either abandoned or placed in a shelter by a frustrated owner. So all of the 'homework' you do in preparation for your pup's arrival will benefit you both. The more informed you are, the more you will know what to expect and the better equipped you will be to handle the ups and downs of raising a puppy. Hopefully, everyone in the household is willing to do his part in raising and caring for the pup. The anticipation of owning a dog often brings a lot of promises from excited family members: 'I will walk him every day,' 'I will feed him,' 'I will housebreak him,' etc., but these things take time and effort, and promises can easily be forgotten once the novelty of the new pet has worn off.

more than accommodating and anxious to sell you one. That breeder will charge you as much as any established breeder. The novice breeder isn't going to interrogate you and your family about your intentions with the puppy, the environment and training you can provide, etc. That breeder will be nowhere to be found when your poorly bred, badly adjusted four-pawed monster starts to growl and spit up at midnight or eat the family cat!

When searching for a pup, always be prepared with a list of questions to determine if the breeder is knowledgeable and responsible in their breeding activities.

- Ask for The Kennel Club registrations on the sire and dam.
- Ask for hip clearance certification on both parents.
- Be sure to view and visit with the dam. Frequently the sire is not on the premises. Both parents should be over two years of age, the dam should not be over seven or eight.
- Ask how often the dam is bred. One litter a year is the maximum. A bitch should never be bred every season. There are no exceptions to this breeding principle.
- See that the premises are clean within reason, allowing that a litter of pups creates a continuous supply of digested food.

reputation is much more important than convenience of location. Do not be overly impressed by breeders who run brag advertisements in the presses about their stupendous champions and working lines. The real quality breeders are quiet and unassuming. You hear about them at the dog trials and shows, by word of mouth. You may be well advised to avoid the novice who lives only a few miles away. The local novice breeder, trying so hard to get rid of that first litter of puppies, is

• Check for fleas and observe the condition of other dogs on the premises. They should all be clean and appear happy and stable, their living areas well-maintained.

• Check the pedigree for champions. Titles in a pedigree are your only assurance that the parents and ancestors were animals of quality.

• Find out if the breeder attends dog shows, obedience trials or field trials with her dogs. Experienced breeders are usually involved in some activity in the dog world.

• Ask if the breeder is a member of the Weimaraner Club or other dog organisations.

• Find out if the pups have been checked by a veterinary surgeon, had their first shots (at about 5 or 6 weeks of age), and if their health records reflect that information.

You should be assertive when interviewing any breeder offering her pups for sale. Conversely, expect the breeder to be equally interested in you as a potential owner of one of her pups. Responsible breeders screen their buyers and try to place their pups with people who understand and care about the breed.

Puppy Selection

Your selection of a good puppy can be determined by your needs. A show potential or a good pet? It is your choice. Every puppy, however, should be of good

temperament. Although show-quality puppies are bred and raised with emphasis on physical conformation, responsible breeders strive for equally good temperament. Do not buy from a breeder who concentrates solely on physical beauty at the expense of personality.

Most Weimaraners live for 12 to 13 years of age, so you are beginning a long-term relationship. The time and effort you invest in finding a good breeder and a dog that suits your needs and personality will reward you and your dog for years to come.

While health considerations in the Weimaraner are not

DOCUMENTATION

Two important documents you will get from the breeder are the pup's pedigree and registration certificate. The breeder should register the litter and each pup with The Kennel Club, and it is necessary for you to have the paperwork if you plan on showing or breeding in the future.

Make sure you know the breeder's intentions on which type of registration he will obtain for the pup. There are limited registrations which may prohibit the dog from being shown, bred or from competing in non-conformation trials such as Working or Agility if the breeder feels that the pup is not of sufficient quality to do so. There is also a type of registration that will permit the dog in non-conformation competition only.

On the reverse side of the registration certificate, the new owner can find the transfer section which must be signed by the breeder.

INSURANCE

Many good breeders will offer you insurance with your new puppy, which is an excellent idea. The first few weeks of insurance will probably be covered free of charge or with only minimal cost, allowing you to take up the policy when this expires. If you own a pet dog, it is sensible to take out such a policy as veterinary fees can be high, although routine vaccinations and boosters are not covered. Look carefully at the many options open to you before deciding which suits you best.

nearly as daunting as in some other breeds, socialisation is a breeder concern of immense importance. Since the Weimaraner's temperament can vary from line to line, socialisation is the first and best way to encourage a proper, stable personality.

Choosing a breeder is an important first step in dog ownership. Fortunately, the majority of Weimaraner breeders are devoted to the breed and its well-being. New owners should have little problem finding a reputable breeder who doesn't live on the other side of the country (or in a different country). The Kennel Club is able to recommend breeders of quality Weimaraners, as can any local all-breed club or Weimaraner club. Potential owners are encouraged to attend field trials to see the Weimaraners in action, to meet the handlers firsthand and to get an idea of what Weimaraners look like outside a photographer's lens. Provided you approach the handlers when they are not terribly busy with the dogs, most are more than willing to answer questions, recommend breeders and give advice.

CHOOSING YOUR PUPPY

Now that you have contacted and met a breeder or two and made your choice about which breeder is best suited to your needs, it's time to visit the litter. Keep in mind that many top breeders have waiting lists. Sometimes new owners have to wait as long as two years for a puppy. If you are really committed to the breeder whom you've selected, then you will wait (and hope for an early arrival!). If not, you may have to resort to your second or third choice breeder. Don't be too anxious, however. If the breeder doesn't have any waiting list, or any customers, there is probably a good reason. It's no different than visiting a pub with no clientele. The better pubs and restaurants always have a waiting list—and it's usually worth the wait. Besides, isn't a

puppy more important than a pint?

Since you are likely to be choosing a Weimaraner as a pet dog and not a working dog, you simply should select a pup that is friendly and attractive. Weimaraners generally have good-sized litters, so selection is good once you have located a desirable litter. While the basic structure of the breed has litter variation, the temperament may present trouble in certain strains. Beware of the shy or overly aggressive puppy: be especially conscious of the

DID YOU KNOW?

Breeders rarely release puppies until they are eight to ten weeks of age. This is an acceptable age for most breeds of dog, excepting toy breeds, which are not released until around 12 weeks, given their petite sizes. If a

breeder has a puppy that is 12 weeks or more, it is likely well socialised and housetrained. Be sure that it is otherwise healthy before deciding to take it home.

ARE YOU A FIT OWNER?

If the breeder from whom you are buying a puppy asks you a lot of personal questions, do not be insulted. Such a breeder wants to be sure that you will be a fit provider for his puppy.

nervous Weimaraner pup. Don't let sentiment or emotion trap you into buying the runt of the litter.

If you have intentions of your new charge hunting in the field, there are many more considerations. The parents of a future hunting dog should have excellent qualifications, including actual work experience as well as working titles in their pedigrees.

The gender of your puppy is largely a matter of personal taste, although there is a common belief amongst those who work with Weimaraners that bitches are quicker to learn and generally more loving and faithful. Males learn more slowly but retain the lesson longer. The difference in size is noticeable but not great.

Breeders commonly allow visitors to see the litter by around the fifth or sixth week, and puppies leave for their new homes between the eighth and tenth week. Breeders who permit their puppies to leave early are more interested in your pounds than their puppies' well-being. Puppies need to learn the rules of the trade from their dams, and most dams continue teaching the pups manners, and dos and don'ts until around the eighth week. Breeders spend significant amounts of time with the Weimaraner toddlers so that they are able to interact with the 'other species', i.e. humans. Given the long history that dogs and humans have, bonding between the two species is natural but must be nurtured. A well-bred, well-socialised Weimaraner pup wants nothing more than to be near you and please you.

Always check the bite of your selected puppy to be sure

A newborn Weimaraner whose umbilical cord has just been surgically severed. Although most Weimaraners are capable of delivering and caring for their own puppies, it is ideal if a veterinary surgeon can assist in the birthing process.

that it is a scissor bite with the upper teeth closely overlapping the lower teeth. This may not be too noticeable on a young puppy but it is a fairly common problem with certain lines of Weimaraners.

COMMITMENT OF OWNERSHIP

After considering all of these factors, you have most likely already made some very important decisions about selecting your puppy. You have chosen a Weimaraner, which means that you have decided which characteristics you want in a dog and what type of dog will best fit into your family and lifestyle. If you have selected a breeder, you have gone a step further—you have done your research and found a responsible, conscientious person who breeds quality Weimaraners and who should be a reliable source of help as you and your puppy adjust to life together. If you have observed a litter in action, you have obtained a firsthand look at the dynamics of a puppy 'pack' and, thus, you should learn about each pup's individual personality—perhaps you have even found one that particularly appeals to you.

However, even if you have not yet found the Weimaraner puppy of your dreams,

Information...

If you lead an erratic, unpredictable life, with daily or weekly changes in your work requirements, consider the problems of owning a

puppy. The new puppy has to be fed regularly, socialised (loved, petted, handled, introduced to other people) and, most importantly, allowed to visit outdoors for toilet training. As the dog gets older, it can be more tolerant of deviations in its feeding and toilet relief.

observing pups will help you learn to recognise certain behaviour and to determine what a pup's behaviour indicates about his temperament. You will be able to pick out which pups are the leaders, which ones are less outgoing, which ones are confident, which ones are shy, playful, friendly, aggressive, etc. Equally as important, you will learn to recognise what a healthy pup should look and act like. All of these things will help you in your search, and when you find the Weimaraner that was meant for you, you will know it!

Researching your breed, selecting a responsible breeder and observing as many pups as possible are all important steps on the way to dog ownership. It may seem like a lot of effort...and you have not even brought the pup home yet! Remember, though, you cannot be too careful when it comes to deciding on the type of dog you want and finding out about your prospective pup's background. Buying a puppy is not—or should not be—just another whimsical purchase. This is one instance in which you actually do get to choose your own family! You may be thinking

Be certain to meet one or both parents of your prospective puppy before purchase. You can tell a great deal about your puppy's temperament and construction from his dam and sire.

that buying a puppy should be fun—it should not be so serious and so much work. Keep in mind that your puppy is not a cuddly stuffed toy or decorative lawn ornament, but a creature that will become a real member of your family. You will come to realise that, while buying a puppy is a pleasurable and exciting endeavour, it is not something to be taken lightly. Relax...the fun will start when the pup comes home!

Always keep in mind that a puppy is nothing more than a baby in a furry disguise...a baby who is virtually helpless in a human world and who trusts his owner for fulfilment of his basic needs for survival. In addition to water and shelter, your pup needs care, protection, guidance and love. If you are not prepared to commit to this, then you are not prepared to own a dog.

Wait a minute, you say. How hard could this be? All of my neighbours own dogs and they seem to be doing just fine. Why should I have to worry about all of this? Well, you should not worry about it; in fact, you will probably find that once your Weimaraner pup gets used to his new home, he will fall into his place in the family quite naturally. But it never hurts to emphasise the commitment of dog ownership. With some time

and patience, it is really not too difficult to raise a curious and exuberant Weimaraner pup to be a well-adjusted and well-mannered adult dog—a dog that could be your most loyal friend.

PREPARING PUPPY'S PLACE IN YOUR HOME
Researching your breed and finding a breeder are only two aspects of the 'homework' you will have to do before bringing your Weimaraner puppy home. You will also have to prepare your home and family for the new addition. Much as you would prepare a nursery for a newborn baby, you will need to designate a place in your home that will be the puppy's own. How you prepare your home will depend on how much freedom the dog will be allowed. Whatever you decide, you must ensure that he has a place that he can 'call his own.'

When you bring your new puppy into your home, you are bringing him into what will become his home as well. Obviously, you did not buy a puppy so that he could take over your house, but in order for a puppy to grow into a stable, well-adjusted dog, he has to feel comfortable in his surroundings. Remember, he is leaving the warmth and security of his mother and littermates, as well as the familiarity of the

41

Weimaraner

PHOTO COURTESY OF DISKROOM.

Your local pet shop should carry a complete range of crates in various sizes, colours and prices.

pup. Imagine how a small child would feel in the same situation—that is how your puppy must be feeling. It is up to you to reassure him and to let him know, 'Little chap, you are going to like it here!'

CRATE TRAINING TIPS

During crate training, you should partition off the section of the crate in which the pup stays. If he is given too big an area, this will hinder your training efforts. Crate training is based on the fact that a dog does not like to soil his sleeping quarters, so it is ineffective to keep a pup in a crate that is so big that he can eliminate in one end and get far enough away from it to sleep. Also, you want to

make the crate den-like for the pup. Blankets and a favourite toy will make the crate cosy for the small pup; as he grows, you may want to evict some of his 'roommates' to make more room.

It will take some coaxing at first, but be patient. Given some time to get used to it, your pup will adapt to his new home-within-a-home quite nicely.

only place he has ever known, so it is important to make his transition as easy as possible. By preparing a place in your home for the puppy, you are making him feel as welcome as possible in a strange new place. It should not take him long to get used to it, but the sudden shock of being transplanted is somewhat traumatic for a young

WHAT YOU SHOULD BUY

CRATE

To someone unfamiliar with the use of crates in dog training, it may seem like punishment to shut a dog in a crate, but this is not the case at all. Although all breeders do not advocate crate training, more and more breeders and trainers are recommending crates as preferred tools for pet puppies as well as show puppies. Crates are not cruel—crates have many humane and highly effective uses in dog care and training. For example, crate training is a very popular and very successful housebreaking method. A crate can keep your dog safe during travel; and, perhaps most importantly, a crate provides your dog with a place of his own in your home. It serves as a 'doggie bedroom' of sorts—your Weimaraner can curl up in his crate when he wants to sleep or when he just needs a break. Many dogs sleep in their crates overnight. When lined with soft bedding and with a favourite toy placed inside, a crate becomes a cosy pseudo-den for your dog. Like his ancestors, he too will seek out the comfort and retreat of a den—you just happen to be providing him with something a little more luxurious than his early ancestors enjoyed.

Information...

The cost of food must also be mentioned. All dogs need a good quality food with an adequate supply of protein to develop their bones and muscles properly.

Most dogs are not picky eaters but unless fed properly they can quickly succumb to skin problems.

As far as purchasing a crate, the type that you buy is up to you. It will most likely be one of the two most popular types: wire or fibreglass. There are advantages and disadvantages to each type. For example, a wire crate is more open, allowing the air to flow through and affording the dog a view of what is going on around him while a fibreglass crate is sturdier. Both can double as travel crates, providing protection for the dog. The size of the crate is another thing to consider. Puppies do not stay puppies forever—in fact, sometimes it seems as if they grow right before your eyes. A small-sized crate may be fine for a very young Weimaraner pup, but it will not do him much good for

43

Weimaraner

long! Unless you have the money and the inclination to buy a new crate every time your pup has a growth spurt, it is better to get one that will accommodate your dog both as a pup and at full size. A large-sized crate will be necessary for a full-grown Weimaraner, who stands approximately 25 inches high.

Toys, Toys, Toys . . .

With a big variety of dog toys available, and so many that look like they would be a lot of fun for a dog, be careful in your selection. It is amazing what a set of

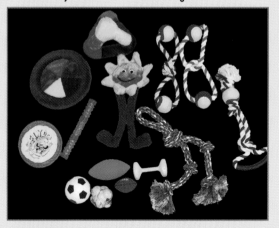

puppy teeth can do to an innocent-looking toy, so, obviously, safety is a major consideration. Be sure to choose the most durable products that you can find. Hard nylon bones and toys are a safe bet, and many of them are offered in different scents and flavours that will be sure to capture your dog's attention. It is always fun to play a game of catch with your dog, and there are balls and flying discs that are specially made to withstand dog teeth.

BEDDING
Veterinary bedding in the dog's crate will help the dog feel more at home and you may also like to pop in a small blanket. This will take the place of the leaves, twigs, etc., that the pup would use in the wild to make a den; the pup can make his own 'burrow' in the crate. Although your pup is far removed from his den-making ancestors, the denning instinct is still a part of his genetic makeup. Second, until you bring your pup home, he has been sleeping amidst the warmth of his mother and litter-mates, and while a blanket is not the same as a warm, breathing body, it still provides heat and something with which to snuggle. You will want to wash your pup's bedding frequently in case he has an accident in his crate, and replace or remove any blanket that becomes ragged and starts to fall apart.

TOYS
Toys are a must for dogs of all ages, especially for curious playful pups. Puppies are the 'children' of the dog world, and what child does not love toys? Chew toys provide enjoyment for both dog and owner—your dog will enjoy playing with his favourite toys, while you will enjoy the fact that they distract him from your expensive shoes

and leather sofa. Puppies love to chew; in fact, chewing is a physical need for pups as they are teething, and everything looks appetising! The full range of your possessions—from old tea towel to Oriental carpet—are fair game in the eyes of a teething pup. Puppies are not all that discerning when it comes to finding something to literally 'sink their teeth into'—everything tastes great!

Weimaraner puppies are fairly aggressive chewers and only the hardest, strongest toys should be offered to them. Breeders advise owners to resist stuffed toys, because they can become de-stuffed in no time. The overly excited pup may ingest the stuffing, which is neither digestible nor nutritious.

FINANCIAL RESPONSIBILITY

Grooming tools, collars, leashes, dog beds and, of course, toys will be an expense to you when you first obtain your pup, and the cost will continue throughout your dog's lifetime. If your puppy damages or destroys your possessions (as most puppies surely will!) or something belonging to a neighbour, you can calculate additional expense. There is also flea and pest control, which every dog owner faces more than once. You must be able to handle the financial responsibility of owning a dog.

Similarly, squeaky toys are quite popular, but must be avoided for the Weimaraner. Perhaps a squeaky toy can be used as an aid in training, but not for free play. If a pup 'disembowels' one of these, the small plastic squeaker inside can be dangerous if swallowed. Monitor the condition of all your pup's toys carefully and get rid of any that have been chewed to the point of becoming potentially dangerous.

Be careful of natural bones, which have a tendency to splinter into sharp, dangerous pieces. Also be careful of rawhide, which can turn into pieces that are easy to swallow or into a mushy mess on your carpet.

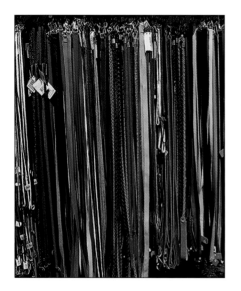

Your pet shop will offer an array of leads from which to choose.

LEAD

A nylon lead is probably the best option as it is the most resistant to puppy teeth should your pup take a liking to chewing on his lead. Of course, this is a habit that should be nipped in the bud, but if your pup likes to chew on his lead he has a very slim chance of being able to chew through the strong nylon. Nylon leads are also lightweight, which is good for a young Weimaraner who is just getting used to the idea of walking on a lead. For everyday walking and safety purposes, the nylon lead is a good choice. As your pup grows up and gets used to walking on the lead, you may want to purchase a flexible lead. These leads allow you to extend the length to give the dog a broader area to explore or to shorten the length to keep the close to you. Of course there are special leads for training purposes, and specially made leather harnesses for working dogs, but these are not necessary for routine walks.

COLLAR

Your pup should get used to wearing a collar all the time since you will want to attach his ID tags to it. Plus, you have to attach the lead to something! A lightweight nylon collar is a good choice; make sure that it fits snugly enough so that the pup cannot wriggle out of it, but is loose enough so that it will not be uncomfortably tight around the pup's neck. You should be able to fit a finger between the pup and the collar. It may take some time for your pup to get used to wearing the collar, but soon he will not even notice that it is there. Choke collars are made for training, but should only be used by an experienced handler.

FOOD AND WATER BOWLS

Your pup will need two bowls, one for food and one for water. You may want two sets of bowls, one for inside and one for outside, depending on where the dog will be fed and where he will be spending most of his time. Stainless steel or sturdy plastic bowls are popular choices. Plastic bowls are more chewable. Dogs tend not to chew on the steel variety, which can be sterilised. It is important to buy sturdy bowls since anything is in danger of being chewed by puppy teeth and you do not want your dog to be constantly chewing apart his bowl (for his safety and for your purse!).

CLEANING SUPPLIES

Until a pup is housetrained you will be doing a lot of cleaning. Accidents will occur, which is

Choosing the Appropriate Collar

The BUCKLE COLLAR is the standard collar used for everyday purpose. Be sure that you adjust the buckle on growing puppies. Check it every day. It can become too tight overnight! These collars can be made of leather or nylon. Attach your dog's identification tags to this collar.

The CHOKE COLLAR is the usual collar recommended for training. It is constructed of highly polished steel so that it slides easily through the stainless steel loop. The idea is that the dog controls the pressure around its neck and he will stop pulling if the collar becomes uncomfortable. Never leave a choke collar on your dog when not training.

The HALTER is for a trained dog that has to be restrained to prevent running away, chasing a cat and the like. Considered the most humane of all collars, it is frequently used on smaller dogs for which collars are not comfortable.

Your local pet shop should offer a complete selection of water and food bowls made of plastic, pottery and stainless steel.

Be a proper citizen and clean up after your dog. Your local pet shop sells equipment that will make the clean-up less troublesome.

okay in the beginning because the puppy does not know any better. All you can do is be prepared to clean up any 'accidents.' Old rags, towels, newspapers and a safe disinfectant are good to have on hand.

BEYOND THE BASICS

The items previously discussed are the bare necessities. You will find out what else you need as you go along—grooming supplies, flea/tick protection, baby gates to partition a room, etc. These things will vary depending on your situation but it is important that you have everything you need to feed and make your Weimaraner comfortable in his first few days at home.

PHOTO COURTESY OF MIKKI PET PRODUCTS.

PUPPY-PROOFING YOUR HOME

Aside from making sure that your Weimaraner will be comfortable in your home, you also have to make sure that your home is safe for your Weimaraner. This means taking precautions that your pup will not get into anything he should not get into and that there is nothing within his reach that may harm him should he sniff it, chew it, inspect it, etc. This probably seems obvious since, while you are primarily concerned with your pup's safety, at the same time you do not want your belongings to be ruined. Breakables should be placed out of reach if your dog is to have full run of the house. If he is to be limited to certain places within the house, keep any potentially dangerous items in the 'off-limits' areas. An electrical cord can pose a danger should the puppy decide to taste it—and who is going to convince a pup that it would not make a great chew toy? Cords should be fastened tightly against the wall. If your dog is going to spend time in a crate, make sure that there is nothing near his crate that he can reach if he sticks his curious little nose or paws through the openings. Just as you would with a child, keep all household cleaners and chemicals where

the pup cannot get to them.

It is also important to make sure that the outside of your home is safe. Of course your puppy should never be unsupervised, but a pup let loose in the garden will want to run and explore, and he should be granted that freedom. Do not let a fence give you a false sense of security; you would be surprised how crafty (and

Information...

You will probably start feeding your pup the same food that he has been getting from the breeder; the breeder should give you a few days' supply to start you off.

Although you should not give your pup too many treats, you will want to have puppy treats on hand for coaxing, training, rewards, etc. Be careful, though, as a small pup's calorie requirements are relatively low and a few treats can add up to almost a full day's worth of calories without the required nutrition.

Weimaraner

Make your new Weimaraner puppy feel at home by offering him time to explore your garden and present him with a nice toy to keep him busy. Always monitor the puppy when he is outdoors.

persistent) a dog can be in working out how to dig under and squeeze his way through small holes, or to jump or climb over a fence. The remedy is to make the fence high enough so that it really is impossible for your dog to get over it (about 3 metres should suffice), and well embedded into the ground. Be sure to repair or secure any gaps in the fence. Check the fence

CHEMICAL TOXINS

Scour your garage for potential puppy dangers. Remove weed killers, pesticides and antifreeze materials. Antifreeze is highly toxic and even a few drops can kill an adult dog. The sweet taste attracts the animal, who will quickly consume it from the floor or curbside.

periodically to ensure that it is in good shape and make repairs as needed; a very determined pup may return to the same spot to 'work on it' until he is able to get through.

FIRST TRIP TO THE VET
You have picked out your puppy, and your home and family are ready. Now all you have to do is collect your Weimaraner from the breeder and the fun begins, right? Well...not so fast. Something else you need to prepare is your pup's first trip to the veterinary surgeon. Perhaps the breeder can recommend someone in the area that specialises in Weimaraners, or maybe you know some other Weimaraner owners who can suggest a good vet. Either way, you should have an appointment arranged for your pup before you pick him up and plan on taking him for an examination before bringing him home.

The pup's first visit will consist of an overall examination to make sure that the pup does not have any problems that are not apparent to the eye. The veterinary surgeon will also set up a schedule for the pup's vaccinations; the breeder will inform you of which ones the pup has already received and the vet can continue from there.

INTRODUCTION TO THE FAMILY

Everyone in the house will be excited about the puppy coming home and will want to pet him and play with him, but it is best to make the introduction low-key so as not to overwhelm the puppy. He is apprehensive already. It is the first time he has been separated from his mother and the breeder, and the ride to your home is likely the first time he has been in a car. The last thing you want to do is smother him. as this will only frighten him further. This is not to say that human contact is not extremely necessary at this stage, because this is the time when a connection between the pup and his human family is formed. Gentle petting and soothing words should help console him, as well as just putting him down and letting him explore on his own (under your watchful eye, of course).

The pup may approach the family members or may busy himself with exploring for a while. Gradually, each person should spend some time with the pup, one at a time, crouching down to get as close to the pup's level as possible and letting him sniff their hands and petting him gently. He definitely needs human attention and he needs to be touched—this is how to form an

Natural Toxins

Examine your grass and garden landscaping before bringing your puppy home. Many varieties of plants have leaves, stems or flowers that are toxic if

ingested, and you can depend on a curious puppy to investigate them. Ask your vet for information on poisonous plants or research them at your library.

immediate bond. Just remember that the pup is experiencing a lot of things for the first time, at the same time. There are new people, new noises, new smells, and new things to investigate: so be gentle, be affectionate, and be as comforting as you can be.

YOUR PUP'S FIRST NIGHT AT HOME

You have travelled home with your new charge safely in his basket or crate. He's been to the

Socialisation

Thorough socialisation includes not only meeting new people but also being introduced to new experiences such as riding in the car, having his coat

brushed, hearing the television, walking in a crowd—the list is endless. The more your pup experiences, and the more positive the experiences are, the less of a shock and the less scary it will be for your pup to encounter new things.

garden and anywhere else he's been permitted. He's eaten his first meal at home and relieved himself in the proper place. He's heard lots of new sounds, smelled new friends and seen more of the outside world than ever before.

That was just the first day! He's worn out and is ready for bed...or so you think!

It's puppy's first night and you are ready to say 'Good night'—keep in mind that this is puppy's first night ever to be sleeping alone. His dam and littermates are no longer at paw's length and he's a bit scared, cold and lonely. Be reassuring to your new family member. This is not the time to spoil him and give in to his inevitable whining.

Puppies whine. They whine to let the others know where they are and hopefully to get company out of it. Place your pup in his new bed or crate in his room and close the door. Mercifully, he may fall asleep without a peep. If the inevitable occurs, ignore the whining: he is fine. Be strong and keep his interest in mind. Do not allow your heart to become guilty and visit the pup. He will fall asleep.

Some breeders suggest moving the crate into your bedroom at night for the first several weeks. Sleeping in your room will not spoil the puppy. It

vet for a thorough check-up; he's been weighed, his papers examined; perhaps he's even been vaccinated and wormed as well. He's met the family, licked the whole family, including the excited children and the less-than-happy cat. He's explored his area, his new bed, the

will make him feel secure and continue the bonding process throughout the night. Beyond that, if the puppy needs to relieve himself during the night, you'll be able to whisk him out immediately. Do not ever give in and remove him from his crate or allow him into bed with you.

Many breeders recommend placing a piece of bedding from his former home in his new bed so that he recognises the scent of his littermates. Others still advise placing a hot water bottle in his bed for warmth. This latter may be a good idea provided the pup doesn't attempt to suckle—he'll get good and wet and may not fall asleep so fast.

Puppy's first night can be somewhat stressful for the pup and his new family. Remember that you are setting the tone of nighttime at your house. Unless you want to play with your pup every evening at 10 p.m., midnight and 2 a.m., don't initiate the habit. Your family will thank you, and so will your pup!

PREVENTING PUPPY PROBLEMS

SOCIALISATION

Now that you have done all of the preparatory work and have helped your pup get accustomed to his new home

TOXIC PLANTS

Many plants can be toxic to dogs. If you see your dog carrying a piece of vegetation in his mouth, approach him in a quiet, disinterested manner, avoid eye contact, pet him and gradually remove the plant from his mouth. Alternatively, offer him a treat and maybe he'll drop the plant on his own accord. Be sure no toxic plants are growing in your own garden.

and family, it is about time for you to have some fun! Socialising your Weimaraner pup gives you the opportunity to show off your new friend, and your pup gets to reap the benefits of being an adorable furry creature that people will want to pet and, in general, think is absolutely precious!

Besides getting to know his new family, your puppy should be exposed to other people, animals and situations, but of course he must not come into close contact with dogs you

Although your pet Weimaraner will probably not be used as a working dog, don't be surprised to see him exhibit instinctive traits.

DID YOU KNOW?

It will take at least two weeks for your puppy to become accustomed

to his new surroundings. Give him lots of love, attention, handling, frequent opportunities to relieve himself, a diet he likes to eat and a place he can call his own.

don't know well until his course of injections is fully complete. This will help him become well adjusted as he grows up and less prone to being timid or fearful of the new things he will encounter. Your pup's socialisation began at the breeder's but now it is your responsibility to continue it. The socialisation he receives up until the age of 16-20 weeks is the most critical, as this is the time when he forms his impressions of the outside world. Be especially careful during the eight-to-ten-week period, also known as the fear period. The interaction he receives during this time should be gentle and reassuring. Lack of socialisation can manifest itself in fear and aggression as the dog grows up. He needs lots of human contact, affection, handling and exposure to other animals.

Once your pup has received his necessary vaccinations, feel free to take him out and about (on his lead, of course). Walk him around the neighbourhood, take him on your daily errands, let people pet him, let him meet other dogs and pets, etc. Puppies do not have to try to make friends; there will be no shortage of people who will want to introduce themselves. Just make sure that you carefully supervise each meeting. If the neighbourhood children want to say hello, for example, that is great—children and pups most often make great companions. Sometimes an excited child can unintentionally handle a pup too roughly, or an overzealous pup can playfully nip a little too hard. You want to make socialisation experiences positive ones. What a pup learns during this very formative stage will affect his attitude toward future encounters. You want your dog to be comfortable around everyone. A pup that has a bad experience with a child may grow up to be a dog that is shy around or aggressive towards children.

CONSISTENCY IN TRAINING

Dogs, being pack animals, naturally need a leader, or else they try to establish dominance in their packs. When you bring a dog into your family, the choice of who becomes the leader and who becomes the 'pack' is entirely up to you! Your pup's intuitive quest for dominance, coupled with the fact that it is nearly impossible to look at an adorable Weimaraner pup, with his 'puppy-dog' eyes and his too-big-for his-head-still-floppy ears, and not cave in, give the pup almost an unfair advantage in getting the upper hand! A pup will definitely test the waters to see what he can and cannot do. Do not give in to those pleading eyes—stand your ground when it comes to disciplining the pup and make sure that all family members do the same. It will only confuse the pup when Mother tells him to get off the sofa when he is used to sitting up there with Father to watch the nightly

DID YOU KNOW?

The majority of problems that are commonly seen in young pups will disappear as your dog gets older. However, how you deal with problems when he is

young will determine how he reacts to discipline as an adult dog. It is important to establish who is boss (hopefully it will be you!) right away when you are first bonding with your dog. This bond will set the tone for the rest of your life together.

Weimaraner

Visiting or participating in a Weimaraner competition enables you to compare the quality of your dog with other Weimaraners. It's possible to discuss behavioural and other problems you encounter with fellow breed owners at the shows.

news. Avoid discrepancies by having all members of the household decide on the rules before the pup even comes home...and be consistent in enforcing them! Early training shapes the dog's personality, so you cannot be unclear in what you expect.

COMMON PUPPY PROBLEMS

The best way to prevent puppy problems is to be proactive in stopping an undesirable behaviour as soon as it starts. The old saying 'You can't teach an old dog new tricks' does not necessarily hold true, but it is true that it is much easier to discourage bad behaviour in a young developing pup than to wait until the pup's bad behaviour becomes the adult dog's bad habit. There are some problems that are especially prevalent in puppies as they develop.

NIPPING

As puppies start to teethe, they feel the need to sink their teeth into anything available... unfortunately that includes your fingers, arms, hair, and toes. You may find this behaviour cute for the first five seconds...until you feel just how sharp those puppy teeth are. This is something you want to discourage immediately and consistently with a firm 'No!' (or whatever number of firm 'No's' it takes for him to understand that you mean business). Then replace your finger with an appropriate chew toy. While this behaviour is merely annoying when the dog is young, it can become dangerous as your Weimaraner's adult teeth grow in and his jaws develop, and he continues to think it is okay to gnaw on human appendages. This is a sporting breed with a natural tendency to chew and nip. Your Weimaraner does not mean any harm with a friendly nip, but he also does not know his own strength.

CRYING/WHINING

Your pup will often cry, whine, whimper, howl or make some type of commotion when he is left alone. This is basically his way of calling out for attention to make sure that you know he is there and that you have not forgotten about him. He feels insecure when he is left alone, when you are out of the house and he is in his crate or when you are in another part of the house and he cannot see you. The noise he is making is an expression of the anxiety he feels at being alone, so he needs to be taught that being alone is okay. You are not actually training the dog to stop making noise, you are training him to feel comfortable when he is alone and thus removing the need for him to make the noise. This is where the crate with cosy bedding and a toy comes in handy. You want to know that he is safe when you are not there to supervise, and you know that he will be safe in his crate rather than roaming freely about the house. In order for the pup to stay in his crate without making a fuss, he needs to be comfortable in his crate. On that

DID YOU KNOW?

Taking your dog from the breeder to your home in a car can be a very uncomfortable experience for both of you. The puppy will have been taken from his warm, friendly, safe environment and brought into a strange new environment. An environment that moves! Be prepared for loose bowels, urination, crying, whining and even fear biting. With proper love and encouragement when you arrive home, the stress of the trip should quickly disappear.

note, it is extremely important that the crate is never used as a form of punishment, or the pup will have a negative association with the crate.

Accustom the pup to the crate in short, gradually increasing time intervals in which you put him in the crate, maybe with a treat, and stay in the room with him. If he cries or makes a fuss, do not go to him, but stay in his sight. Gradually he will realise that staying in his crate is all right without your help, and it will not be so traumatic for him when you are not around. You may want to leave the radio on softly when you leave the house; the sound of human voices may be comforting to him.

DIETARY AND FEEDING CONSIDERATIONS

Today the choices of food for your Weimaraner are many and varied. There are simply dozens of brands of food in all sorts of flavours and textures, ranging from puppy diets to those for seniors. There are even hypoallergenic and low-calorie diets available. Because your Weimaraner's food has a bearing on coat, health and temperament, it is essential that the most suitable diet is selected for a Weimaraner of his age. It is fair to say, however, that even dedicated owners can be somewhat perplexed by the enormous range of foods available. Only understanding what is best for your dog will help you reach a valued decision.

Dog foods are produced in three basic types: dried, semi-moist and tinned. Dried foods are useful for the cost-conscious for overall they tend to be less expensive than semi-moist or tinned. These contain the least fat and the most preservatives. In general tinned foods are made up of 60–70 percent water, while semi-moist ones often contain so much sugar that they are perhaps the least preferred by owners, even though their dogs seem to like them.

When selecting your dog's diet, three stages of development must be considered: the puppy stage, the adult stage and the senior or veteran stage.

PUPPY STAGE

Puppies instinctively want to suck milk from their mother's teats and a normal puppy will exhibit this behaviour from just a few moments following birth. If puppies do not attempt to suckle within the first half-hour or so, they should be encouraged to do

FOOD TIPS

You must store your dried dog food carefully. Open packages of dog food quickly lose their vitamin value, usually within 90 days of being opened. Mould spores and vermin could also contaminate the food.

so by placing them on the nipples, having selected ones with plenty of milk. This early milk supply is important in providing colostrum to protect the puppies during the first eight to ten weeks of their lives. Although a mother's milk is much better than any milk formula, despite there being some excellent ones available, if the puppies do not feed you will have to feed them yourself. For those with less experience, advice from a veterinary surgeon is important so that you feed not only the right quantity of milk but that of correct quality, fed at suitably frequent intervals, usually every two hours during the first few days of life.

Puppies should be allowed to nurse from their mothers for about the first six weeks, although from the third or fourth week you will have begun to introduce small portions of suitable solid food. Most breeders like to introduce alternate milk and meat meals initially, building up to weaning time.

By the time the puppies are seven or a maximum of eight weeks old, they should be fully weaned and fed solely on a proprietary puppy food. Selection of the most suitable, good-quality diet at this time is essential for a puppy's fastest growth rate is during the first year of life. Avoid puppy food with high fat content as excess weight on a puppy can be harmful. Veterinary surgeons

Food Preference

Selecting the best dried dog food is difficult. There is no majority consensus amongst veterinary scientists as to the value of nutrient analyses

(protein, fat, fibre, moisture, ash, cholesterol, minerals, etc.). All agree that feeding trials are what matters, but you also have to consider the individual dog. Its weight, age, activity and what pleases its taste, all must be considered. It is probably best to take the advice of your veterinary surgeon. Every dog's dietary requirements vary, even during the lifetime of a particular dog.

If your dog is fed a good dried food, it does not require supplements of meat or vegetables. Dogs do appreciate a little variety in their diets so you may choose to stay with the same brand, but vary the flavour. Alternatively you may wish to add a little flavoured stock to give a difference to the taste.

are usually able to offer advice in this regard and, although the frequency of meals will have been reduced over time, only when a young dog has reached the age of about 10 months should an adult diet be fed.

Puppy and junior diets should be well balanced for the needs of your dog, so that except in certain circumstances additional vitamins, minerals and proteins will not be required.

ADULT DIETS

A dog is considered an adult when it has stopped growing, so in general the diet of a Weimaraner can be changed to an adult one at about 10 to 12 months of age, possibly sooner. Again you should rely upon your

veterinary surgeon or dietary specialist to recommend an acceptable maintenance diet. Major dog food manufacturers specialise in this type of food, and it is just necessary for you to select the one best suited to your dog's needs. Active dogs may have different requirements than sedate dogs.

SENIOR DIETS

As dogs get older, their metabolism changes. The older dog usually exercises less, moves more slowly and sleeps more. This change in lifestyle and physiological performance requires a change in diet. Since these changes take place slowly, they might not be recognisable. What is easily recognisable is weight gain. By continuing to feed your dog an adult-maintenance diet when it is slowing down metabolically, your dog will gain weight. Obesity in an older dog compounds the health problems that already accompany old age.

As your dog gets older, few of his organs function up to par. The kidneys slow down and the intestines become less efficient. These age-related factors are best handled with a change in diet and a change in feeding schedule to give smaller portions that are more easily digested.

There is no single best diet for every older dog. While many dogs do well on light or senior diets,

GRAIN-BASED DIETS

Some less expensive dog foods are based on grains and other plant proteins. Whilst these products may appear to be attractively priced, many breeders prefer a diet based on animal proteins and believe that they are more conducive to your dog's health. Many grain-based diets rely on soy protein that may cause flatulence (passing gas).

There are many cases, however, when your dog might require a special diet. These special requirements should only be recommended by your veterinary surgeon.

other dogs do better on puppy diets or other special premium diets such as lamb and rice. Be sensitive to your senior Weimaraner's diet and this will help control other problems that may arise with your old friend.

WATER

Just as your dog needs proper nutrition from his food, water is an essential 'nutrient' as well. Water keeps the dog's body properly hydrated and promotes normal function of the body's systems. During housebreaking it is necessary to keep an eye on how much water your

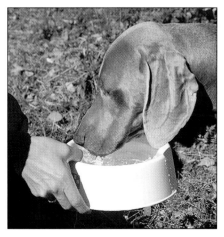

You must supply your Weimaraner with clean, fresh water. Whether he is resting indoors or playing outdoors, be sure that drinking water is available.

Weimaraner is drinking, but once he is reliably trained he should have access to clean fresh water at all times. Make sure that the dog's water bowl is clean, and change the water often, making sure that water is always available for your dog, especially if you feed dried food.

EXERCISE

All dogs require some form of exercise, regardless of breed and the Weimaraner is a gundog with an abundance of energy and enthusiam. A sedentary lifestyle is as harmful to a dog as it is to a person. The Weimaraner is a very active breed that enjoys exercise, but you don't have to be an Olympic athlete! Long daily walks, play sessions in the garden, or letting the dog run free in the garden under your supervision are sufficient forms of exercise for the Weimaraner. For

DID YOU KNOW?

A good test for proper diet is the colour, odour and firmness of your dog's stool. A healthy dog usually

produces three semi-hard stools per day. The stools should have no unpleasant odour. They should be the same colour from excretion to excretion.

What are you feeding your dog?

Read the label on your dog food. Many dog foods only advise what 50–55% of the contents are, leaving the other 45% in doubt.

1.3% Calcium
1.6% Fatty Acids
4.6% Crude Fibre
11% Moisture
14% Crude Fat
22% Crude Protein
45.5% ? ? ?

those who are more ambitious, you will find that your Weimaraner also enjoys long runs, an occasional hike or even a swim! Bear in mind that an overweight dog should never be suddenly over-exercised; instead he should be allowed to increase exercise slowly. Not only is exercise essential to keep the dog's body fit, it is essential to his mental well being. A bored dog will find something to do, which often manifests itself in some type of destructive behaviour. In this sense, it is essential for the owner's mental well-being as well!

GROOMING

BRUSHING

A natural bristle brush or a hound glove can be used for regular routine brushing. Daily brushing is effective for removing dead hair and stimulating the dog's natural oils to add shine and a healthy look to the coat. Both the Shorthair and Longhair require a five-minute once-over to keep them looking their shiny best, with the Longhair requiring more regular attention. Regular grooming sessions are also a good way to spend time with your dog. Many dogs grow to like the feel of being brushed and will enjoy the daily routine.

DOG FOOD TIPS

Dog food must be at room temperature, neither too hot nor too cold. Fresh water, changed daily and served in a clean bowl, is mandatory, especially when feeding dried food.

Never feed your dog from the table while you are eating. Never feed your dog left-overs from your own meal. They usually contain too much fat and too much seasoning.

Dogs must chew their food. Hard pellets are excellent; soups and slurries are to be avoided.

Don't add left-overs or any extras to normal dog food. The normal food is usually balanced and adding something extra destroys the balance.

Except for age-related changes, dogs do not require dietary variations. They can be fed the same diet, day after day, without their becoming ill.

Depending on the length of your Weimaraner's coat, your need for various brushes and combs will vary. Obviously, you can discuss your grooming needs with your breeder or local pet shop keeper.

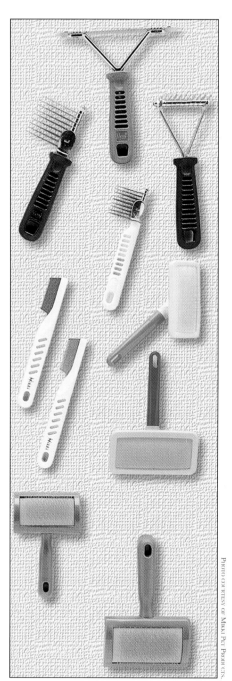

PHOTO COURTESY OF MIKKI PET PRODUCTS.

BATHING

Dogs do not need to be bathed as often as humans, but regular bathing is essential for healthy skin and a healthy, shiny coat. Again, like most anything, if you accustom your pup to being bathed as a puppy, it will be second nature by the time he grows up. You want your dog to be at ease in the bath or else it could end up a wet, soapy, messy ordeal for both of you!

Brush your Weimaraner thoroughly before wetting his coat. This will get rid of most loose hair and dandruff, which are harder to remove when the coat is wet. Make that your dog has a good non-slip surface to stand on. Begin by wetting the

GROOMING EQUIPMENT

How much grooming equipment you purchase will depend on how much grooming you are going to do. Here are some basics:

- Natural bristle brush
- Slicker brush
- Metal comb
- Scissors
- Blaster
- Rubber mat
- Dog shampoo
- Spray hose attachment
- Ear cleaner
- Cotton wipes
- Towels
- Nail clippers

dog's coat. A shower or hose attachment is necessary for thoroughly wetting and rinsing the coat. Check the water temperature to make sure that it is neither too hot nor too cold.

Next, apply shampoo to the dog's coat and work it into a good lather. You should purchase a shampoo that is made for dogs. Do not use a product made for human hair. Wash the head last; you do not want shampoo to drip into the dog's eyes while you are washing the rest of his body. Work the shampoo all the way down to the skin. You can use this opportunity to check the skin for any bumps, bites or other abnormalities. Do not neglect any area of the body— get all of the hard-to-reach places.

Once the dog has been thoroughly shampooed, he requires an equally thorough

Train your Weimaraner to sit calmly for his brushing session. Here's Gunner, owned by Mary and Charles McGee, enjoying his grooming time.

These three illustrations show different types of gloves with which you can keep your Weimaraner's coat healthy and free of dust and loose hairs. The photo in the centre is a type of glove brush that has very short comb-like projections to loosen dead hair and stimulate the dog's skin.

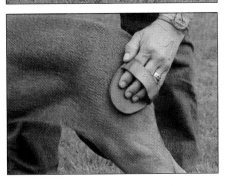

Bathing Tips

The use of human soap products like shampoo, bubble bath and hand soap can be damaging to a dog's coat and skin. Human products are too strong and remove the

protective oils coating the dog's hair and skin (making him water-resistant). Use only shampoo made especially for dogs and you may like to use a medicated shampoo, which will always help to keep external parasites at bay.

EAR CLEANING

The ears should be kept clean and any excess hair inside the ear should be carefully cut. Ears can be cleaned with a cotton wipe and special cleaner or ear powder made especially for dogs. Be on the lookout for any signs of infection or ear mite infestation. If your Weimaraner has been shaking his head or scratching at his ears frequently, this usually indicates a problem. If his ears have an unusual odour, this is a sure sign of mite infestation or infection, and a signal to have his ears checked by the veterinary surgeon.

NAIL CLIPPING

Your Weimaraner should be accustomed to having his nails trimmed at an early age, since it will be part of your maintenance routine throughout his life. Not only does it look nicer, but long nails can be sharp if they scratch someone unintentionally. Also, a long nail has a better chance of ripping and bleeding, or causing the feet to spread. A good rule of thumb is that if you can hear your dog's nails clicking on the floor when he walks, his nails are too long.

Before you start cutting, make sure you can identify the 'quick' in each nail. The quick is a blood vessel that runs through the centre of each nail and grows rather close to the end. It will

rinsing. Shampoo left in the coat can be irritating to the skin. Protect his eyes from the shampoo by shielding them with your hand and directing the flow of water in the opposite direction. You should also avoid getting water in the ear canal. Be prepared for your dog to shake out his coat— you might want to stand back, but make sure you have a hold on the dog to keep him from running through the house.

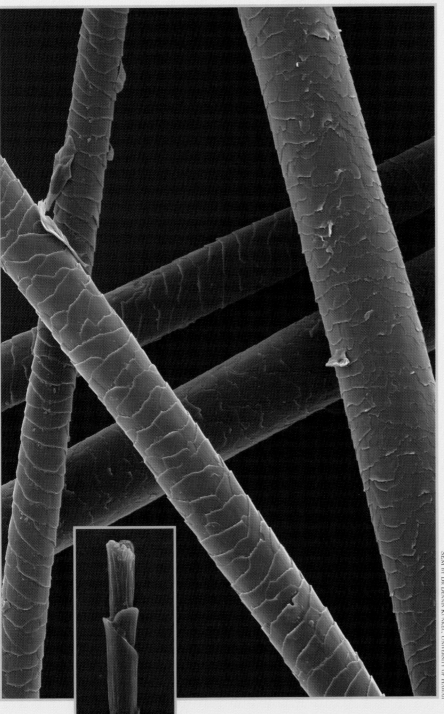

Normal hairs of a dog enlarged 200 times original size. The cuticle (outer covering) is clean and healthy. Unlike human hair that grows from the base, dog's hair also grows from the end, as shown in the inset. Scanning electron micrographs by Dr Dennis Kunkel, University of Hawaii.

BATHING TIP

Once you are sure that the dog is thoroughly rinsed, squeeze the excess water out of the coat with your hand and dry him with a heavy towel. You may choose to use a blaster on his coat or just let it dry naturally. In cold weather, never allow your dog outside with a wet coat.

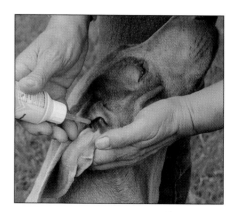

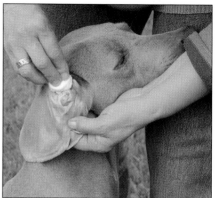

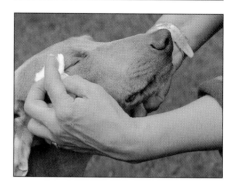

There are 'dry bath' products on the market, which are sprays and powders intended for spot cleaning, that can be used between regular baths, if necessary. They are not substitutes for regular baths, but they are easy to use for touch-ups as they do not require rinsing.

Top: Applying an ear powder or liquid cleaner. **Centre:** Removing the medication applied in the top photo with a soft, cotton wipe. Inspect for excess hair growth. **Bottom:** Tear stains can usually be removed with a cotton wipe.

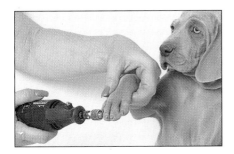

Grinding the Weimaraner's nails is a sensible way to keep nails filed. Introduce the puppy to this procedure early on.

bleed if accidentally cut, which will be quite painful for the dog as it contains nerve endings. Keep some type of clotting agent on hand, such as a styptic pencil or styptic powder (the type used for shaving). This will stop the bleeding quickly when applied to the end of the cut nail. Do not panic if you cut the quick, just stop the bleeding and talk soothingly to your dog. Once he has calmed down, move on to the next nail. It is better to clip a little at a time, particularly with black-nailed dogs.

Hold your pup steady as you begin trimming his nails; you do

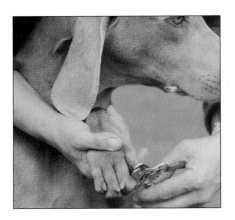

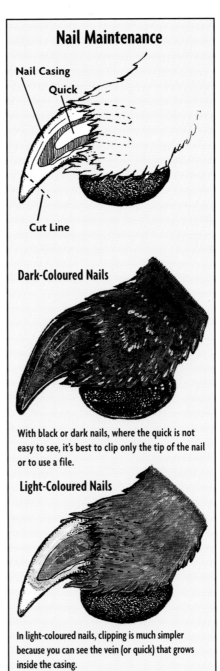

Nail Maintenance

Nail Casing

Quick

Cut Line

Dark-Coloured Nails

With black or dark nails, where the quick is not easy to see, it's best to clip only the tip of the nail or to use a file.

Light-Coloured Nails

In light-coloured nails, clipping is much simpler because you can see the vein (or quick) that grows inside the casing.

Special nail clippers are available from your local pet supplier. Start trimming the nails when your Weimaraner is still a puppy so he will be accustomed to the procedure.

69

not want him to make any sudden movements or run away. Talk to him soothingly and stroke him as you clip. Holding his foot in your hand, simply take off the end of each nail in one quick clip. You can purchase nail clippers that are specially made for dogs; you can probably find them wherever you buy pet or grooming supplies.

DID YOU KNOW?

A dog that spends a lot of time outside on a hard surface, such as cement or pavement, will have his nails naturally worn down and may not need to have them trimmed as often, except maybe in

the colder months when he is not outside as much. Regardless, it is best to get your dog accustomed to this procedure at an early age so that he is used to it. Some dogs are especially sensitive about having their feet touched, but if a dog has experienced it since he was young, he should not be bothered by it.

TRAVELLING WITH YOUR DOG

CAR TRAVEL

You should accustom your Weimaraner to riding in a car at an early age. You may or may not take him in the car often, but at the very least he will need to go to the vet and you do not want these trips to be traumatic for the dog or troublesome for you. The safest way for a dog to ride in the car is in his crate. If he uses a crate in the house, you can use the same crate for travel, if your vehicle can accommodate it. Put the pup in the crate and see how he reacts. If the puppy seems uneasy, you can have a passenger hold him on his lap while you drive but you will need to find another solution by the time your dog is fully grown. Another option is a specially made safety harness for dogs, which straps the dog in much like a seat belt. Do not let the dog roam loose in the vehicle—this is very dangerous! If you should stop short, your dog can be thrown and injured. If the dog starts climbing on you and pestering you while you are driving, you will not be able to concentrate on the road. It is an unsafe situation for everyone—human and canine.

For long trips, be prepared to stop to let the dog relieve himself. Bring along whatever you need to clean up after him. You should take along some paper kitchen towels and perhaps some old towelling for use should he have an accident in the car or suffer from travel sickness.

AIR TRAVEL

While it is possible to take a dog on a flight within Britain, this is fairly unusual and advance permission is always required. The dog will be required to travel in a fibreglass crate and you should always check in advance with the airline regarding specific requirements. To help the dog be at ease, put one of his favourite toys in the crate with him. Do not feed the dog for at least six hours before the trip to minimise his need to relieve himself. However, certain regulations specify that water must always be made available to the dog in the crate.

Make sure your dog is properly identified and that your contact information appears on his ID tags and on his crate. Animals travel in a different area of the plane from human passen-

TRAVEL TIP

When travelling, never let your dog off-lead in a strange area. Your dog could run away out of fear or decide to chase a passing squirrel or cat or

simply want to stretch his legs without restriction—you might never see your canine friend again.

gers, so every rule must be strictly followed in order to prevent the risk of getting separated from your dog.

BOARDING

So you want to take a family holiday—and you want to include *all* members of the family. You would probably make arrangements for accommodation ahead of time anyway, but this is especially important when travelling with a dog. You do not want to make an overnight stop at the only place around for miles and find out that they do not allow

TRAVEL TIP

If you are going on a long motor trip with your dog, be sure the hotels are dog friendly. Many hotels do not accept dogs. Also take along some ice that can be thawed and offered to your dog if he becomes overheated. Most dogs like to lick ice.

71

TRAVEL TIP

For international travel you will have to make arrangements well in advance (perhaps months), as countries' regulations pertaining to bringing in animals differ. There may be special health certificates and/or vaccinations that your dog will need before taking the trip; sometimes this has to be done within a certain time frame. In rabies-free countries, you will need to bring proof of the dog's rabies vaccination and there may be a quarantine period upon arrival.

dogs. Also, you do not want to reserve a place for your family without confirming that you are travelling with a dog because if it is against their policy you may not have a place to stay.

Alternatively, if you are travelling and choose not to bring your Weimaraner, you will have to make arrangements for him while you are away. Some options are to take him to a neighbour's house to stay while you are gone, to have a trusted neighbour stop by often or stay at your house, or bring your dog to a reputable boarding

Shop around for boarding facilities before you actually need to use them. Visit the facilities and confirm the cleanliness, attitude of the attendants, and the space available for the dogs to exercise.

kennel. If you choose to board him at a kennel, you should visit in advance to see the facilities provided, how clean they are and where the dogs are kept. Talk to some of the employees and see how they treat the dogs—do they spend time with the dogs, play with them, exercise them, etc.? Also find out the kennel's policy on vaccinations and what they require. This is for all of the dogs' safety, since when dogs are kept together, there is a greater risk of diseases being passed from dog to dog.

IDENTIFICATION

Your Weimaraner is your valued companion and friend. That is why you always keep a close eye on him and you have made sure that he cannot escape from the garden or wriggle out of his collar and run away from you. However, accidents can happen and there may come a time when your dog unexpectedly gets separated from you. If this unfortunate event

TRAVEL TIP

Never leave your dog alone in the car. In hot weather your dog can die from the high temperature inside a closed vehicle; even a car parked in the shade can heat up very quickly. Leaving the window open is dangerous as well since the dog can hurt himself trying to get out.

IDENTIFICATION

If your dog gets lost, he is not able to ask for directions home.

Identification tags fastened to the collar give important information—the dog's name, the owner's name, the owner's address and a telephone

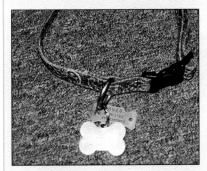

number where the owner can be reached. This makes it easy for whomever finds the dog to contact the owner and arrange to have the dog returned. An added advantage is that a person will be more likely to approach a lost dog who has ID tags on his collar; it tells the person that this is somebody's pet rather than a stray. This is the easiest and fastest method of identification provided that the tags stay on the collar and the collar stays on the dog.

should occur, the first thing on your mind will be finding him. Proper identification, including an ID tag, a tattoo and possibly a microchip, will increase the chances of his being returned to you safely and quickly.

Information...

Weimaraners are known to be sensitive dogs who learn best with gentle but consistent teaching methods. They thrive on praise and knowing that they have pleased

their masters. Never physically abuse your dog or hit him with your hand, foot or newspaper. That will only teach the dog to be afraid of you.

Living with an untrained dog is a lot like owning a piano that you do not know how to play— it is a nice object to look at but it does not do much more than that to bring you pleasure. Now try taking piano lessons and suddenly the piano comes alive and brings forth magical sounds and rhythms that set your heart singing and your body swaying.

The same is true with your Weimaraner. Any dog is a big responsibility and if not trained sensibly may develop unacceptable behaviour that annoys you or could even cause family friction.

To train your Weimaraner, you may like to enrol in an obedience class. Teach him good manners as you learn how and why he behaves the way he does. Find out how to communicate with your dog and how to recognise and understand his communications with you. Suddenly the dog takes on a new role in your life—he is clever, interesting, well behaved and fun to be with. He demonstrates his bond of devotion to you daily. In other words, your Weimaraner does wonders for your ego because he constantly reminds you that you are not only his leader, you are his hero!

Those involved with teaching dog obedience and counselling owners about their dogs' behaviour have discovered some interesting facts about dog ownership. For example, training dogs when they are puppies results in the highest rate of success in developing well-mannered and well-adjusted adult dogs. Training an older dog, from six months to six years of age, can produce almost equal results providing that the owner accepts the dog's slower rate of learning capability and is willing to work patiently to help the dog succeed at developing to his fullest potential. Unfortunately, many owners of untrained adult dogs lack the patience factor, so they do not persist until their dogs are successful at learning particular behaviours.

Training a puppy aged 10 to 16 weeks (20 weeks at the most) is like working with a dry sponge in a pool of water. The pup soaks up whatever you show him and constantly looks for more things to do and learn. At this early age, his body is not yet producing hormones, and therein lies the reason for such a high rate of success. Without hormones, he is focused on his owners and not particularly interested in investigating other places, dogs, people, etc. You

CONSISTENCY PAYS OFF

Dogs need consistency in their feeding schedule, exercise and toilet breaks and in the verbal commands you use. If you use 'Stay' on Monday and 'Stay here, please' on Tuesday, you will confuse your dog. Don't demand perfect behaviour during training classes and then let him have the run of the house the rest of the day. Above all, lavish praise on your pet consistently every time he does something right. The more he feels he is pleasing you, the more willing he will be to learn.

are his leader: his provider of food, water, shelter and security. He latches onto you and wants to stay close. He will usually follow you from room to room, will not let you out of his sight when you are outdoors with him, and will respond in like manner to the people and animals you encounter. If you greet a friend warmly, he will be happy to greet the person as well. If, however, you are hesitant, even anxious, about the approach of a stranger, he will respond accordingly.

Once the puppy begins to produce hormones, his natural curiosity emerges and he begins to investigate the world around him. It is at this time when you may notice that the untrained dog begins to wander away from

What a wonderful bond there is between an owner and a well-behaved canine companion!

followed faithfully, you may expect positive results that will prove rewarding to both you and your dog.

Whether your new charge is a puppy or a mature adult, the methods of teaching and the techniques we use in training basic behaviours are the same. After all, no dog, whether puppy or adult, likes harsh or inhumane methods. All creatures, however, respond favourably to gentle motivational methods and sincere praise and encouragement. Now let us get started.

HOUSEBREAKING

You can train a puppy to relieve itself wherever you choose, but this must be somewhere suitable. You should bear in mind from the outset that when your puppy is old enough to go out in public places, any canine deposits must be removed at once. You will always have to

you and even ignore your commands to stay close.

There are usually classes within a reasonable distance of the owner's home, but you can also do a lot to train your dog yourself. Sometimes there are classes available but the tuition is too costly. Whatever the circumstances, the solution to the problem of lack of lesson availability lies within the pages of this book.

This chapter is devoted to helping you train your Weimaraner at home. If the recommended procedures are

DID YOU KNOW?

To a dog's way of thinking, your hands are like his mouth in terms of a defence mechanism. If you squeeze him too tightly, he might just bite you because that would be his normal response. This is not aggressive biting and, although all biting should be discouraged, you need the discipline in learning how to handle your dog.

carry with you a small plastic bag or 'poop-scoop.'

Outdoor training includes such surfaces as grass, mud, soil or earth and cement. Indoor training usually means training your dog to newspaper.

When deciding on the surface and location that you will want your Weimaraner to use, be sure it is going to be permanent. Training your dog to grass and then changing your mind two months later is extremely difficult for both dog and owner.

Next, choose the command you will use each and every time you want your puppy to void. 'Be quick' and 'Hurry up' are examples of commands commonly used by dog owners.

Get in the habit of giving the puppy your chosen relief command before you take him out. That way, when he becomes an adult, you will be able to determine if he wants to go out when you ask him. A confirmation will be signs of interest, wagging his tail, watching you intently, going to the door, etc.

PUPPY'S NEEDS

Puppy needs to relieve himself after play periods, after each meal, after he has been sleeping and any time he indicates that he is looking for a place to urinate or defecate.

Practice Makes Perfect!

• Have training lessons with your dog every day in several short segments—three to five times a day for a few minutes at a time is ideal.
• Do not have long practice sessions. The dog will become easily bored.
• Never practise when you are tired, ill, worried or in an otherwise negative mood. This will transmit to the dog and may have an adverse effect on its performance.

Think fun, short and above all POSITIVE! End each session on a high note, rather than a failed exercise, and make sure to give a lot of praise. Enjoy the training and help your dog enjoy it, too.

The urinary and intestinal tract muscles of very young puppies are not fully developed. Therefore, like human babies, puppies need to relieve themselves frequently.

HOUSEBREAKING TIP

Most of all, be consistent. Always take your dog to the same location, always use the same command, and always have him on lead when he is in

his relief area, unless a fenced-in garden is available.

By following the Success Method, your puppy will be completely housetrained by the time his muscle and brain development reach maturity. Keep in mind that small breeds usually mature faster than large breeds, but all puppies should be trained by six months of age.

Take your puppy out often—every hour for an eight-week-old, for example, and always immediately after sleeping and eating. The older the puppy, the less often he will need to relieve himself. Finally, as a mature healthy adult, he will require only three to five relief trips per day.

HOUSING

Since the types of housing and control you provide for your puppy has a direct relationship to the success of housetraining, we consider the various aspects of both before we begin training.

Bringing a new puppy home and turning him loose in your house can be compared to turning a child loose in a sports arena and telling the child that the place is all his! The sheer enormity of the place would be too much for him to handle.

Instead, offer the puppy clearly defined areas where he can play, sleep, eat and live. A room of the house where the family gathers is the most obvious choice. Puppies are social animals and need to feel a part of the pack right from the start. Hearing your voice, watching you whilst you are

HOW MANY TIMES A DAY?

AGE	RELIEF TRIPS
To 14 weeks	10
14–22 weeks	8
22–32 weeks	6
Adulthood (dog stops growing)	4

These are estimates, of course, but they are a guide to the MINIMUM opportunities a dog should have each day to relieve itself.

doing things and smelling you nearby are all positive reinforcers that he is now a member of your pack. Usually a family room, the kitchen or a nearby adjoining breakfast area is ideal for providing safety and security for both puppy and owner.

Within that room there should be a smaller area which the puppy can call his own. An alcove, a wire or fibreglass dog crate or a fenced (not boarded!) corner from which he can view the activities of his new family will be fine. The size of the area or crate is the key factor here. The area must be large enough for the puppy to lie down and stretch out as well as stand up without rubbing his head on the top, yet small enough so that he cannot relieve himself at one end and sleep at the other without coming into contact with his droppings until fully trained to relieve himself outside.

Dogs are, by nature, clean animals and will not remain close to their relief areas unless forced to do so. In those cases, they then become dirty dogs and usually remain that way for life.

The designated area should be lined with clean bedding and a toy. Water must always be available, in a non-spill container.

HOUSEBREAKING TIP

Do not carry your dog to his toilet area. Lead him there on a leash or, better yet, encourage him to follow

you to the spot. If you start carrying him to his spot, you might end up doing this routine forever and your dog will have the satisfaction of having trained YOU.

CONTROL

By control, we mean helping the puppy to create a lifestyle pattern that will be compatible to that of his human pack (YOU!). Just as we guide little children to learn our way of life, we must show the puppy when it is time to play, eat, sleep, exercise and even entertain himself.

Your puppy should always sleep in his crate. He should

CANINE DEVELOPMENT SCHEDULE

It is important to understand how and at what age a puppy develops into adulthood. If you are a puppy owner, consult the following Canine Development Schedule to determine the stage of development your puppy is currently experiencing. This knowledge will help you as you work with the puppy in the weeks and months ahead.

Period	Age	Characteristics
FIRST TO THIRD	BIRTH TO SEVEN WEEKS	Puppy needs food, sleep and warmth, and responds to simple and gentle touching. Needs mother for security and disciplining. Needs littermates for learning and interacting with other dogs. Pup learns to function within a pack and learns pack order of dominance. Begin socialising with adults and children for short periods. Begins to become aware of its environment.
FOURTH	EIGHT TO TWELVE WEEKS	Brain is fully developed. Needs socialising with outside world. Remove from mother and littermates. Needs to change from canine pack to human pack. Human dominance necessary. Fear period occurs between 8 and 16 weeks. Avoid fright and pain.
FIFTH	THIRTEEN TO SIXTEEN WEEKS	Training and formal obedience should begin. Less association with other dogs, more with people, places, situations. Period will pass easily if you remember this is pup's change-to-adolescence time. Be firm and fair. Flight instinct prominent. Permissiveness and over-disciplining can do permanent damage. Praise for good behaviour.
JUVENILE	FOUR TO EIGHT MONTHS	Another fear period about 7 to 8 months of age. It passes quickly, but be cautious of fright and pain. Sexual maturity reached. Dominant traits established. Dog should understand sit, down, come and stay by now.

NOTE: THESE ARE APPROXIMATE TIME FRAMES. ALLOW FOR INDIVIDUAL DIFFERENCES IN PUPPIES.

also learn that, during times of household confusion and excessive human activity such as at breakfast when family members are preparing for the day, he can play by himself in relative safety and comfort in his designated area. Each time you leave the puppy alone, he should understand exactly where he is to stay. You can gradually increase the time he is left alone to get him used to it. Puppies are chewers. They cannot tell the difference between lamp cords, television wires, shoes, table legs, etc. Chewing into a television wire, for example, can be fatal to the puppy whilst a shorted wire can start a fire in the house.

If the puppy chews on the arm of the chair when he is alone, you will probably discipline him angrily when you get home. Thus, he makes the association that your coming home means he is going to be punished. (He will not remember chewing the chair and is incapable of making the association of the discipline with his naughty deed.)

Other times of excitement, such as family parties, etc., can be fun for the

A wire crate is popular for use in the home. Do not put water in the crate until the pup is fully housetrained, as this will invite 'accidents' when the pup is crated.

puppy providing he can view the activities from the security of his designated area. He is not underfoot and he is not being fed all sorts of titbits that will probably cause him stomach distress, yet he still feels a part of the fun.

SCHEDULE

A puppy should be taken to his relief area each time he is released from his designated area, after meals, after a play session, when he first awakens in the morning (at age eight weeks, this can mean 5 a.m.!).

All puppies, whether male or female, squat to urinate. As males mature, they will eventually lift their legs.

The puppy will indicate that he's ready 'to go' by circling or sniffing busily—do not misinterpret these signs. For a puppy less than ten weeks of age, a routine of taking him out every hour is necessary. As the puppy grows, he will be able to wait for longer periods of time.

Keep trips to his relief area short. Stay no more than five or six minutes and then return to the house. If he goes during that time, praise him lavishly and take him indoors immediately. If he does not, but he has an

accident when you go back indoors, pick him up immediately, say 'No! No!' and return to his relief area. Wait a few

THE SUCCESS METHOD

1 Tell the puppy 'Crate time!' and place him in the crate with a small treat (a piece of cheese or half of a biscuit). Let him stay in the crate for five minutes while you are in the same room. Then release him and praise lavishly. Never release him when he is fussing. Wait until he is quiet before you let him out.

2 Repeat Step 1 several times a day.

3 The next day, place the puppy in the crate as before. Let him stay there for ten minutes. Do this several times.

4 Continue building time in five-minute increments until the puppy

stays in his crate for 30 minutes with you in the room. Always take him to his relief area after prolonged periods in his crate.

5 Now go back to Step 1 and let the puppy stay in his crate for five minutes, this time while you are out of the room.

6 Once again, build crate time in five-minute increments with you out of the room. When the puppy will stay willingly in his crate (he may even fall asleep!) for 30 minutes with you out of the room, he will be ready to stay in it for several hours at a time.

6 Steps to Successful Crate Training

minutes, then return to the house again. Never hit a puppy or rub his face in urine or excrement when he has an accident!

Once indoors, put the puppy in his crate until you have had time to clean up his accident. Then release him to the family area and watch him more closely than before. Chances are, his accident was a result of your not picking up his signal or waiting too long before offering him the opportunity to relieve himself. Never hold a grudge against the puppy for accidents.

Let the puppy learn that going outdoors means it is time to relieve himself, not play. Once trained, he will be able to play indoors and out and still differentiate between the times for play versus the times for relief.

Help him develop regular hours for naps, being alone, playing by himself and just resting, all in his crate. Encourage him to entertain himself whilst you are busy with your activities. Let him learn that having you near is comforting, but it is not your main purpose in life to provide him with undivided attention.

Each time you put a puppy in his own area, use the same command, whatever suits best. Soon, he will run to his crate or special area when he hears you say those words.

Crate training provides safety for you, the puppy and the home. It also provides the puppy with a feeling of security, and that helps the puppy achieve self-confidence and clean habits.

Remember that one of the primary ingredients in housetraining your puppy is control. Regardless of your lifestyle, there will always be occasions when you will need to have a place where your dog can stay and be happy and safe.

TRAINING TIP

Be authoritative when giving your dog commands. Do not issue commands when lying on the floor or lying on

your back on the sofa. If you are on your hands and knees when you give a command, your dog will think you are positioning yourself to play.

DID YOU KNOW?

As puppies become more and more expensive, especially those puppies of high quality for showing and/or breeding, they have a greater chance of being stolen. The usual collar dog tag is, of course, easily removed. But there are two techniques that have become widely used for identification.

The puppy microchip implantation involves the injection of a small microchip, about the size of a corn kernel, under the skin of the dog. If your dog shows up at a clinic or shelter, or is offered for resale under less than savoury circumstances, it can be positively identified by the microchip. The microchip is scanned and a registry quickly identifies you as the owner. This is not only protection against theft, but should the dog run away or go chasing a squirrel and get lost, you have a fair chance of getting it back.

Tattooing is done on various parts of the dog, from its belly to its cheeks. The number tattooed can be your telephone number or any other number which you can easily memorise. When professional dog thieves see a tattooed dog, they usually lose interest in it. Both microchipping and tattooing can be done at your local veterinary clinic. For the safety of our dogs, no laboratory facility or dog broker will accept a tattooed dog as stock.

Training is the answer for now and in the future.

In conclusion, a few key elements are really all you need for a successful housetraining method—consistency, frequency, praise, control and supervision. By following these procedures with a normal, healthy puppy, you and the puppy will soon be past the stage of 'accidents' and ready to move on to a full and rewarding life together.

ROLES OF DISCIPLINE, REWARD AND PUNISHMENT

Discipline, training one to act in accordance with rules, brings order to life. It is as simple as that. Without discipline, particularly in a group society, chaos reigns supreme and the group will eventually perish. Humans and canines are social animals and need some form of discipline in order to function effectively. They must procure food, protect their home base and their young and reproduce to keep the species going.

If there were no discipline in the lives of social animals, they would eventually die from starvation and/or predation by other stronger animals.

In the case of domestic canines, dogs need discipline in their lives in order to understand how their pack (you and other family members) functions and how they must act in order to survive.

A large humane society in a highly populated area recently surveyed dog owners regarding their satisfaction with their relationships with their dogs. People who had trained their dogs were 75% more satisfied with their pets than those who had never trained their dogs.

Dr Edward Thorndike, a psychologist, established *Thorndike's Theory of Learning*, which states that a behaviour that results in a pleasant event tends to be repeated. A behaviour that results in an unpleasant event tends not to be repeated. It is this theory on which training methods are based today. For example, if you manipulate a dog to perform a specific behaviour and reward

Weimaraners have ideas all their own. Teach your Weimaraner the established house rules before he becomes accustomed to asserting his opinion!

him for doing it, he is likely to do it again because he enjoyed the end result.

Occasionally, punishment, a penalty inflicted for an offence, is necessary. The best type of punishment often comes from an outside source. For example, a child is told not to touch the stove because he may get burned. He disobeys and touches the stove. In doing so, he receives a burn. From that time on, he respects the heat of the stove and avoids contact with it. Therefore, a behaviour that results in an unpleasant event tends not to be repeated.

A good example of a dog learning the hard way is the dog who chases the house cat. He is

Training a puppy requires patience and time. While an adult dog may assist in the teaching by setting a proper example, he can also be a distraction to the pup.

told many times to leave the cat alone, yet he persists in teasing the cat. Then, one day he begins chasing the cat but the cat turns and swipes a claw across the dog's face, leaving him with a painful gash on his nose. The final result is that the dog stops chasing the cat.

TRAINING EQUIPMENT

COLLAR AND LEAD

For a Weimaraner the collar and lead that you use for training must be one with which you are easily able to work, not too heavy for the dog and perfectly safe.

The lead you choose must be safe and comfortable for the dog, yet durable enough for an athletic breed.

TREATS

Have a bag of treats on hand. Something nutritious and easy to swallow works best. Use a soft treat, a chunk of cheese or a piece of cooked chicken rather than a dry biscuit. By the time the dog has finished chewing a dry treat, he will forget why he is being rewarded in the first place! Using food rewards will not teach a dog to beg at the table—the only way to teach a dog to beg at the table is to give

Weimaraners are easily motivated by treats. The use of treats makes training more manage-able and interesting for the dog.

him food from the table. In training, rewarding the dog with a food treat will help him associate praise and the treats with learning new behaviours that obviously please his owner.

TRAINING BEGINS: ASK THE DOG A QUESTION

In order to teach your dog anything, you must first get his attention. After all, he cannot learn anything if he is looking away from you with his mind on something else.

To get his attention, ask

The great outdoors can be a great distraction for a curious Weimaraner. Training sessions should be held in a fenced area where the dog's focus is on the lesson.

DID YOU KNOW?

Dogs are the most honourable animals in existence. They consider another species (humans) as their own. They interface with you. You are their leader. Puppies perceive children to be on their level; their actions around small children are different from their behaviour around their adult masters.

TRAINING TIP

Your dog is actually training you at the same time you are training him. Dogs do things to get attention. They usually repeat whatever succeeds in getting your attention.

him, 'School?' and immediately walk over to him and give him a treat as you tell him 'Good dog.' Wait a minute or two and repeat the routine, this time with a treat in your hand as you approach within a foot of the dog. Do not go directly to him, but stop about a foot short of him and hold out the treat as you ask, 'School?' He will see you approaching with a treat in your hand and most likely begin walking toward you. As you meet, give him the treat and praise again.

The third time, ask the question, have a treat in your hand and walk only a short distance toward the dog so that he must walk almost all the way to you. As he reaches you, give him the treat and praise again.

By this time, the dog will probably be getting the idea that if he pays attention to you, especially when you ask that question, it will pay off in treats and fun activities for him. In other words, he learns that 'school' means doing enjoyable

things with you that result in treats and positive attention for him.

Remember that the dog does not understand your verbal language, he only recognises sounds. Your question translates to a series of sounds for him, and those sounds become the signal to go to you and pay attention; if he does, he will get to interact with you plus receive treats and praise.

THE BASIC COMMANDS

TEACHING SIT

Now that you have the dog's attention, attach his lead and hold it in your left hand and a food treat in your right. Place your food hand at the dog's nose and let him lick the treat but not take it from you. Say 'Sit' and slowly raise your food hand from in front of the dog's nose up over his head so that he is looking at the ceiling. As he bends his head upward, he will have to bend his knees to maintain his balance. As he bends his knees, he will assume a sit position. At that point, release the food treat and praise lavishly with comments such as 'Good dog! Good sit!', etc. Remember to always praise enthusiastically, because dogs relish verbal praise from their owners and feel so proud of themselves whenever they

DID YOU KNOW?

Dogs are as different from each other as people are. What works for one dog may not work for another. Have an open mind. If one method of training is unsuccessful, try another.

accomplish a behaviour.

You will not use food forever in getting the dog to obey your commands. Food is only used to teach new behaviours, and once the dog knows what you want when you give a specific command, you will wean him off of the food treats but still maintain the

verbal praise. After all, you will always have your voice with you, and there will be many times when you have no food rewards but expect the dog to obey.

TEACHING DOWN
Teaching the down exercise is easy when you understand how the dog perceives the down position, and it is very difficult when you do not. Dogs perceive the down position as a submissive one, therefore teaching the down exercise using a forceful method can sometimes make the dog develop such a fear of the down that he either runs

For the well-trained Weimaraner, agility trials may be an option. Weimaraners excel on the jumps, hurdles, tunnels and other obstacles in the course.

Learning the SIT exercise is not difficult for the Weimaraner and is the most basic command. For dogs who do not respond to the treat prompt, a little push on the hindquarters may be necessary.

slowly lower the food hand to the dog's front feet. When the food hand reaches the floor, begin moving it forward along the floor in front of the dog. Keep talking softly to the dog, saying things like, 'Do you want this treat? You can do this, good dog.' Your reassuring tone of voice will help calm the dog as he tries to follow the food hand in order to get the treat.

When the dog's elbows touch the floor, release the food and praise softly. Try to get the dog to maintain that down position for several seconds

away when you say 'Down' or he attempts to snap at the person who tries to force him down.

Have the dog sit close alongside your left leg, facing in the same direction as you are. Hold the lead in your left hand and a food treat in your right. Now place your left hand lightly on the top of the dog's shoulders where they meet above the spinal cord. Do not push down on the dog's shoulders; simply rest your left hand there so you can guide the dog to lie down close to your left leg rather than to swing away from your side when he drops.

Now place the food hand at the dog's nose, say 'Down' very softly (almost a whisper), and

DID YOU KNOW?

A dog in jeopardy never lies down. He stays alert on his feet because instinct tells him that he may have to run away or fight for his survival.

Therefore, if a dog feels threatened or anxious, he will not lie down. Consequently, it is important to have the dog calm and relaxed as he learns the down exercise.

before you let him sit up again. The goal here is to get the dog to settle down and not feel threatened in the down position.

TEACHING STAY
It is easy to teach the dog to stay in either a sit or a down position. Again, we use food and praise during the teaching process as we help the dog to understand exactly what it is that we are expecting him to do.

To teach the sit/stay, start with the dog sitting on your left side as before and hold the lead in your left hand. Have a food treat in your right hand and place your food hand at the dog's nose. Say 'Stay' and step out on your right foot to stand directly in front of the dog, toe

You can teach the STAY exercise when the dog is disciplined to SIT or DOWN.

to toe, as he licks and nibbles the treat. Be sure to keep his head facing upward to maintain the sit position. Count to five and then swing around to stand next to the dog again with him on your left. As soon as you get back to the original position, release the food and praise lavishly.

To teach the down/stay, do the down as previously described. As soon as the dog lies down, say 'Stay' and step out on your right foot just as you did in the sit/stay. Count to

Teaching the STAY exercise can utilise both vocal and hand signals.

five and then return to stand beside the dog with him on your left side. Release the treat and praise as always.

Within a week or ten days, you can begin to add a bit of distance between you and your dog when you leave him. When you do, use your left hand open with the palm facing the dog as a stay signal, much the same as the hand signal a police officer uses to stop traffic at an intersection. Hold the food treat in your right hand as before, but this time the food is not touching the dog's nose. He will watch the food hand and quickly learn that he is going to get that treat as soon as you return to his side.

When you can stand 1 metre away from your dog for 30 seconds, you can then begin building time and distance in both stays. Eventually, the dog can be expected to remain in the stay position for prolonged periods of time until you return to him or call him to you. Always praise lavishly when he stays.

TEACHING COME

If you make teaching 'come' an enjoyable experience, you should never have a 'student' that does not love the game or that fails to come when called. The secret, it seems, is never to teach the word 'come.'

At times when an owner most wants his dog to come when called, the owner is likely upset or anxious and he allows these feelings to come through in the tone of his voice when he calls his dog. Hearing that desperation in his owner's voice, the dog fears the results

Weimaraners love to fetch and will try to retrieve almost anything. This water-worthy Weimaraner is retrieving a huge, floating stick.

of going to him and therefore either disobeys outright or runs in the opposite direction. The secret, therefore, is to teach the dog a game and, when you want him to come to you, simply play the game. It is practically a no-fail solution!

To begin, have several members of your family take a few food treats and each go into a different room in the house. Take turns calling the dog, and each person should celebrate the dog's finding him with a treat and lots of happy praise. When a person calls the dog, he is actually inviting the dog to find him and get a treat as a reward for 'winning.'

A few turns of the 'Where are you?' game and the dog will understand that everyone is playing the game and that each person has a big celebration awaiting his success at locating them. Once he learns to love the game, simply calling out 'Where are you?' will bring him running from wherever he is when he hears that all-important question.

The come command is recognised as one of the most important things to teach a dog, but there are trainers who work with thousands of dogs and never teach the actual word 'Come.' Yet these dogs will race to respond to a person who uses the dog's name followed by

The Golden Rule

The golden rule of dog training is simple. For each 'question' (command), there is only one correct answer (reaction). One command = one reaction.

Keep practising the command until the dog reacts correctly without hesitating. Be repetitive but not monotonous. Dogs get bored just as people do!

'Where are you?' For example, a woman has a 12-year-old companion dog who went blind, but who never fails to locate her owner when asked, 'Where are you?'

Children particularly love to play this game with their dogs. Children can hide in smaller places like a shower or bath,

TRAINING TIP

Teach your dog to HEEL in an enclosed area. Once you think the dog will obey reliably and you want

to attempt advanced obedience exercises such as off-lead heeling, test him in a fenced-in area so he cannot run away.

pulling. It takes time and patience on the owner's part to succeed at teaching the dog that he (the owner) will not proceed unless the dog is walking calmly beside him. Pulling out ahead on the lead is definitely not acceptable.

Begin with holding the lead in your left hand as the dog sits beside your left leg. Move the loop end of the lead to your right hand but keep your left hand short on the lead so it keeps the dog in close next to you.

Say 'Heel' and step forward on your left foot. Keep the dog close to you and take three steps. Stop and have the dog sit next to you in what we now call the 'heel position.' Praise verbally, but do not touch the dog. Hesitate a moment and begin again with 'Heel,' taking three steps and stopping, at which point the dog is told to sit again.

Your goal here is to have the dog walk those three steps without pulling on the lead. When he will walk calmly beside you for three steps without pulling, increase the number of steps you take to five. When he will walk politely beside you whilst you take five steps, you can increase the length of your walk to ten steps. Keep increasing the length of your stroll until the dog will

behind a bed or under a table. The dog needs to work a little bit harder to find these hiding places, but when he does he loves to celebrate with a treat and a tussle with a favourite youngster.

Teaching Heel
Heeling means that the dog walks beside the owner without

THINK BEFORE YOU BARK!

Dogs are sensitive to their master's moods and emotions. Use your voice wisely when communicating with your dog. Never raise your voice at your dog unless you are angry and trying to correct him. 'Barking' at your dog can become as meaningless as 'dogspeak' is to you. Think before you bark!

walk quietly beside you without pulling as long as you want him to heel. When you stop heeling, indicate to the dog that the exercise is over by verbally praising as you pet him and say 'OK, good dog.' The 'OK' is used as a release word meaning that the exercise is finished and the dog is free to relax.

If you are dealing with a dog who insists on pulling you around, simply 'put on your brakes' and stand your ground until the dog realises that the two of you are not going anywhere until he is beside you and moving at your pace, not his. It may take some time just standing there to convince the dog that you are the leader and you will be the one to decide on the direction and speed of your travel.

Each time the dog looks up at you or slows down to give a slack lead between the two of

you, quietly praise him and say, 'Good heel. Good dog.' Eventually, the dog will begin to respond and within a few days he will be walking politely beside you without pulling on the lead. At first, the training sessions should be kept short and very positive; soon the dog will be able to walk nicely with you for increasingly longer distances. Remember also to give the dog free time and the

RULES TO OBEY

If you want to be successful in training your dog, you have four rules to obey yourself:
1. Develop an understanding of how a dog thinks.

2. Do not blame the dog for lack of communication.
3. Define your dog's personality and act accordingly.
4. Have patience and be consistent.

Training Tip

If you begin teaching the heel by taking long walks and letting the dog pull you along, he misinterprets this action as an acceptable form

of taking a walk. When you pull back on the lead to counteract his pulling, he reads that tug as a signal to pull even harder!

opportunity to run and play when you have finished heel practice.

WEANING OFF FOOD IN TRAINING

Food is used in training new behaviours. Once the dog understands what behaviour goes with a specific command, it is time to start weaning him off the food treats. At first, give a treat after each exercise. Then, start to give a treat only after every other exercise. Mix up the times when you offer a food reward and the times when you only offer praise so that the dog will never know when he is going to receive both food and praise and when he is going to receive only praise. This is called a variable ratio reward system and it proves successful because there is always the chance that the owner will produce a treat, so the dog never stops trying for that reward. No matter what, ALWAYS give verbal praise.

OBEDIENCE CLASSES

It is a good idea to enrol in an obedience class if one is available in your area. If yours is a show dog, ringcraft classes would be more appropriate. Many areas have dog clubs that offer basic obedience training as well as preparatory classes for obedience competition. There are also local dog trainers who offer similar classes.

At obedience trials, dogs can earn titles at various levels of competition. The beginning levels of competition include basic behaviours such as sit, down, heel, etc. The more advanced levels of competition include jumping, retrieving, scent discrimination and signal work. The advanced levels require a dog and owner to put a lot of time and effort into their training and the titles that can be earned at these levels of competition are very prestigious.

OTHER ACTIVITIES FOR LIFE

Whether a dog is trained in the structured environment of a class or alone with his owner at home, there are many activities that can bring fun and rewards to both owner and dog once they have mastered basic control.

Teaching the dog to help out around the home, in the garden or on the farm provides great satisfaction to both dog and owner. In addition, the dog's help makes life a little easier for his owner and raises his stature as a valued companion to his family. It helps give the dog a purpose by occupying his mind and providing an outlet for his energy.

Backpacking is an exciting and healthy activity that the dog can be

taught without assistance from more than his owner. The exercise of walking and climbing is good for man and dog alike, and the bond that they develop together is priceless.

If you are interested in participating in organised competition with your Weimaraner, there are activities other than obedience in which you and your dog can become involved. Agility is a popular and enjoyable sport where dogs run through an obstacle course that includes various jumps, tunnels and other exercises to test the dog's speed and coordination. The owners run through the course beside their dogs to give commands and to guide them through the course. Although competitive, the focus is on fun—it's fun to do, fun to watch and great exercise.

There are many Weimaraner clubs that have various types of competitions and activities. Enquire of your local club to become involved in these events.

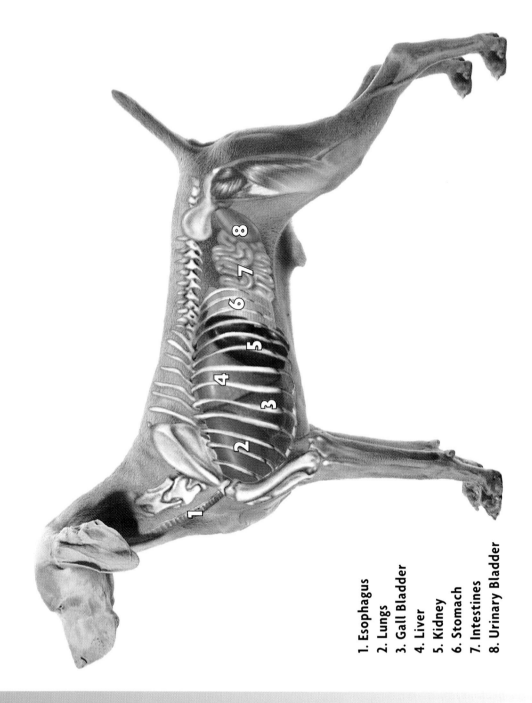

1. Esophagus
2. Lungs
3. Gall Bladder
4. Liver
5. Kidney
6. Stomach
7. Intestines
8. Urinary Bladder

Internal Organs of the Weimaraner

HEALTH CARE OF YOUR
WEIMARANER

Dogs suffer many of the same physical illnesses as people. They might even share many of the same psychological problems. Since people usually know more about human diseases than canine maladies, many of the terms used in this chapter will be familiar but not necessarily those used by veterinary surgeons. We will use the term *x-ray*, instead of the more acceptable term *radiograph*. We will also use the familiar term *symptoms* even though dogs don't have symptoms, which are verbal descriptions of the patient's feelings; dogs have *clinical signs*. Since dogs can't speak, we have to look for clinical signs...but we still use the term symptoms in this book.

As a general rule, medicine is practised. That term is not arbitrary. Medicine is a constantly changing art as we learn more and more about genetics, electronic aids (like CAT scans) and daily laboratory advances. There are many dog maladies, like canine hip dysplasia, which are not universally treated in the same manner. Some veterinary surgeons opt for surgery more often than others do.

SELECTING A VETERINARY SURGEON

Your selection of a veterinary surgeon should not be based upon personality (as most are) but upon their convenience to your home. You want a vet who is close because you might have emergencies or need to make multiple visits for treatments. You want a vet who has services that you might require such as a boarding kennel and grooming facilities, as well as sophisticated pet supplies and a good reputation for ability and responsive-

Tail docking has become controversial in recent years. In Britain, only a qualified veterinary surgeon is permitted to perform this procedure. In years past, breeders were able to take care of the task themselves.

First Aid at a Glance

Burns
Place the affected area under cool water; use ice if only a small area is burnt.

Bee/Insect bites
Apply ice to relieve swelling; antihistamine dosed properly.

Animal bites
Clean any bleeding area; apply pressure until bleeding subsides; go to the vet.

Spider bites
Use cold compress and a pressurised pack to inhibit venom's spreading.

Antifreeze poisoning
Induce vomiting with hydrogen peroxide. Seek *immediate* veterinary help!

Fish hooks
Removal best handled by vet; hook must be cut in order to remove.

Snake bites
Pack ice around bite; contact vet quickly; identify snake for proper antivenin.

Car accident
Move dog from roadway with blanket; seek veterinary aid.

Shock
Calm the dog, keep him warm; seek immediate veterinary help.

Nosebleed
Apply cold compress to the nose; apply pressure to any visible abrasion.

Bleeding
Apply pressure above the area; treat wound by applying a cotton pack.

Heat stroke
Submerge dog in cold bath; cool down with fresh air and water; go to the vet.

Frostbite/Hypothermia
Warm the dog with a warm bath, electric blankets or hot water bottles.

Abrasions
Clean the wound and wash out thoroughly with fresh water; apply antiseptic.

 Remember: an injured dog may attempt to bite a helping hand from fear and confusion. Always muzzle the dog before trying to offer assistance.

ness. There is nothing more frustrating than having to wait a day or more to get a response from your veterinary surgeon.

All veterinary surgeons are licensed and their diplomas and/or certificates should be displayed in their waiting rooms. There are, however, many veterinary specialities that usually require further studies and internships. There are specialists in heart problems (veterinary cardiologists), skin problems (veterinary dermatologists), teeth and gum problems (veterinary dentists), eye problems (veterinary ophthalmologists), x-rays (veterinary radiologists), and surgeons who have specialities in bones, muscles or other organs. Most veterinary surgeons do routine surgery such as neutering, stitching up wounds and docking tails for those breeds in which such is required for show purposes. When the problem affecting your dog is serious, it is not unusual or impudent to get another medical opinion,

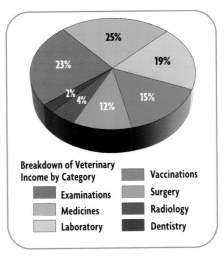

A typical American vet's income, categorised according to services provided. This survey dealt with small-animal practices.

DID YOU KNOW?

Male dogs are neutered. The operation removes the testicles and requires that the dog be anaesthetised. Recovery takes about one week. Females are spayed. This is major surgery and it usually takes a bitch two weeks to recover.

although in Britain you are obliged to advise the vets concerned about this. You might also want to compare costs amongst several veterinary surgeons. Sophisticated health care and veterinary services can be very costly. Don't be bashful about discussing these costs with your veterinary surgeon or his (her) staff. It is not infrequent that important decisions are based upon financial considerations.

PREVENTATIVE MEDICINE

It is much easier, less costly and more effective to practise preventative medicine than to fight bouts of illness and disease. Properly bred puppies come from parents that were selected based upon their genetic disease profile. Their mothers should have been vaccinated, free of all internal and external parasites and properly

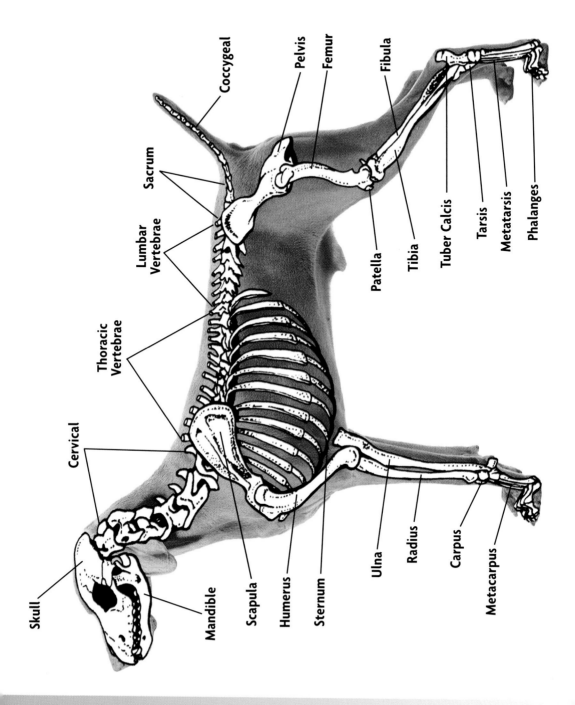

Coccygeal

Pelvis

Femur

Fibula

Sacrum

Tuber Calcis

Tarsis

Metatarsis

Phalanges

Lumbar
Vertebrae

Patella

Tibia

Thoracic
Vertebrae

Cervical

Skull

Mandible

Scapula

Humerus

Sternum

Ulna

Radius

Carpus

Metacarpus

Skeletal Structure of the Weimaraner

nourished. For these reasons, a visit to the veterinary surgeon who cared for the dam (mother) is recommended. The dam can pass on disease resistance to her puppies, which can last for eight to ten weeks. She can also pass on parasites and many infections. That's why you should visit the veterinary surgeon who cared for the dam.

WEANING TO FIVE MONTHS OLD

Puppies should be weaned by the time they are about two months old. A puppy that remains for at least eight weeks with its mother and littermates usually adapts better to other dogs and people later in its life.

Some new owners have their puppy examined by a veterinary surgeon immediately, which is a good idea. Vaccination programmes usually begin when the puppy is very young.

The puppy will have its teeth examined and have its skeletal conformation and general health checked prior to certification by the veterinary surgeon. Puppies in certain breeds have problems with their kneecaps, eye cataracts and other eye problems, heart murmurs and undescended testicles. They may also have personality problems and your veterinary surgeon might have training in temperament evaluation.

DID YOU KNOW?

Not every dog's ears are the same. Ears that are open to the air are healthier than ears with poor air circulation. Sometimes a dog can

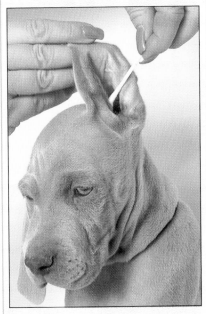

have two differently shaped ears. You should not probe inside your dog's ears. Only clean that which is accessible with a soft cotton wipe.

VACCINATION SCHEDULING

Most vaccinations are given by injection and should only be done by a veterinary surgeon. Both he and you should keep a record of the date of the injection, the identification of the vaccine and the amount given. Some vets give a first vaccination at eight weeks, but most dog breeders prefer the course not to commence until about ten weeks because of negating any antibodies passed on by the dam. The vaccination scheduling is usually based on a two- to three-week lapse. You must take your vet's advice as to when to vaccinate as this may differ according to the vaccine used. Most vaccinations immunise your puppy against viruses.

The usual vaccines contain immunising doses of several different viruses such as distemper, parvovirus, parain-fluenza and hepatitis. There are other vaccines available when the puppy is at risk. You should rely upon professional advice. This is especially true for the booster-shot programme. Most vaccination programmes require a booster when the puppy is a year old and once a year thereafter. In some cases, circumstances may require more frequent immunisations.

Kennel cough, more formally

DID YOU KNOW?

Vaccines do not work all the time. Sometimes dogs are allergic to them and many times the antibodies, which are supposed to be stimulated by the vaccine, just are not produced. You should keep your dog in the veterinary clinic for an hour after it is vaccinated to be sure there are no allergic reactions.

known as tracheobronchitis, is treated with a vaccine that is sprayed into the dog's nostrils. Kennel cough is usually included in routine vaccination, but this is often not so effective as for other major diseases.

FIVE MONTHS TO ONE YEAR OF AGE
Unless you intend to breed or show your dog, neutering the puppy at six months of age is recommended. Discuss this with your veterinary surgeon; most professionals advise neutering the puppy. Neutering has proven to be extremely beneficial to both male and female puppies. Besides eliminating the possibility of pregnancy, it inhibits (but does not prevent) breast cancer in bitches and prostate cancer in male dogs. It is very rare to diagnose breast cancer in a female dog who was spayed at or before about nine months of age before their first heat.

Your veterinary surgeon

DID YOU KNOW?

Your veterinary surgeon will probably recommend that your puppy be vaccinated before you take him outside. There are airborne diseases, parasite eggs in the grass and unexpected visits from other dogs that might be dangerous to your puppy's health.

should provide your puppy with a thorough dental evaluation at six months of age, ascertaining whether all the permanent teeth have erupted properly. A home dental care regimen should be initiated at six months, including brushing weekly and providing good dental devices (such as nylon bones). Regular dental care promotes healthy teeth, fresh breath and a longer life.

ONE TO SEVEN YEARS
Once a year, your grown dog should visit the vet for an examination and vaccination boosters. Some vets recommend blood tests, thyroid level check and dental evaluation to accompany these annual visits. A thorough clinical evaluation by the vet can provide critical background information for your dog. Blood tests are often performed at one year of age, and dental examinations around the third or fourth birthday. In the long run, quality preventive care for your pet can save money, teeth and lives.

SKIN PROBLEMS IN WEIMARANERS
Veterinary surgeons are consulted by dog owners for skin problems

Your Weimaraner's health starts with the health of its parents. If its parents were well kept, healthy and disciplined, your puppy will probably have the same traits.

HEALTH AND VACCINATION SCHEDULE

AGE IN WEEKS:	6TH	8TH	10TH	12TH	14TH	16TH	20-24TH	1 YR
Worm Control	✔	✔	✔	✔	✔	✔	✔	
Neutering								✔
Heartworm*		✔		✔		✔	✔	
Parvovirus	✔		✔		✔		✔	✔
Distemper		✔		✔		✔		✔
Hepatitis		✔		✔		✔		✔
Leptospirosis								✔
Parainfluenza	✔		✔		✔			✔
Dental Examination		✔					✔	✔
Complete Physical		✔					✔	✔
Coronavirus				✔			✔	✔
Kennel Cough	✔							
Hip Dysplasia								✔
Rabies*							✔	

Vaccinations are not instantly effective. It takes about two weeks for the dog's immunization system to develop antibodies. Most vaccinations require annual booster shots. Your veterinary surgeon should guide you in this regard.
*Not applicable in the United Kingdom

more than any other group of diseases or maladies. Dogs' skin is almost as sensitive as human skin and both suffer almost the same ailments (though the occurrence of acne in dogs is rare!). For this reason, veterinary dermatology has developed into a speciality practised by many veterinary surgeons.

Since many skin problems have visual symptoms that are almost identical, it requires the skill of an experienced veterinary dermatologist to identify and cure many of the more severe skin disorders. Pet shops sell many treatments for skin problems but most of the treatments are directed at symptoms and not the underlying problem(s). If your dog is suffering from a skin disorder, you should seek professional assistance as quickly as possible. As with all diseases, the earlier a problem is identified and treated, the more successful is the cure.

PARASITE BITES

Many of us are allergic to insect bites. The bites itch, erupt and may even become infected. Dogs have the same reaction to fleas, ticks and/or mites. When an insect lands on you, you have the chance to whisk it away with your hand. Unfortunately, when our dog is bitten by a flea, tick or mite, it can only scratch it away or bite it. By the time the dog has been bitten, the parasite has done some of its damage. It may also have laid eggs to cause further problems in the near future. The itching from parasite bites is probably due to the saliva injected into the site when the parasite sucks the dog's blood.

AUTO-IMMUNE SKIN CONDITIONS
Auto-immune skin conditions are commonly referred to as being allergic to yourself, whilst allergies are usually inflammatory reactions to an outside stimulus. Auto-immune diseases cause serious damage to the tissues that are involved.

The best known auto-immune disease is lupus, which affects people as well as dogs. The symptoms are variable and may affect the kidneys, bones, blood chemistry and skin. It can be fatal to both dogs and humans, though it is not thought to be transmissible. It is usually successfully treated with cortisone, prednisone or similar corticosteroid, but extensive use of these drugs can have harmful side effects.

DISEASE REFERENCE CHART

	What is it?	What causes it?	Symptoms
Leptospirosis	Severe disease that affects the internal organs; can be spread to people.	A bacterium, which is often carried by rodents, that enters through mucous membranes and spreads quickly throughout the body.	Range from fever, vomiting and loss of appetite in less severe cases to shock, irreversible kidney damage and possibly death in most severe cases.
Rabies	Potentially deadly virus that infects warm-blooded mammals. Not seen in United Kingdom.	Bite from a carrier of the virus, mainly wild animals.	1st stage: dog exhibits change in behaviour, fear. 2nd stage: dog's behaviour becomes more aggressive. 3rd stage: loss of coordination, trouble with bodily functions.
Parvovirus	Highly contagious virus, potentially deadly.	Ingestion of the virus, which is usually spread through the faeces of infected dogs.	Most common: severe diarrhoea. Also vomiting, fatigue, lack of appetite.
Kennel cough	Contagious respiratory infection.	Combination of types of bacteria and virus. Most common: *Bordetella bronchiseptica* bacteria and parainfluenza virus.	Chronic cough.
Distemper	Disease primarily affecting respiratory and nervous system.	Virus that is related to the human measles virus.	Mild symptoms such as fever, lack of appetite and mucous secretion progress to evidence of brain damage, 'hard pad.'
Hepatitis	Virus primarily affecting the liver.	Canine adenovirus type I (CAV-1). Enters system when dog breathes in particles.	Lesser symptoms include listlessness, diarrhoea, vomiting. More severe symptoms include 'blue-eye' (clumps of virus in eye).
Coronavirus	Virus resulting in digestive problems.	Virus is spread through infected dog's faeces.	Stomach upset evidenced by lack of appetite, vomiting, diarrhoea.

Weimaraner

Checking your dog's coat for insect bites, parasite infestation or other irritants should be part of your daily routine. This is especially important with the Weimaraner, who loves to spend time outdoors.

ACRAL LICK GRANULOMA
Weimaraners and many other dogs have a very poorly understood syndrome called acral lick. The manifestation of the problem is the dog's tireless attack at a specific area of the body, almost always the legs. The dog licks so intensively that he removes the hair and skin, leaving an ugly large wound. There is no absolute cure, but corticosteroids are the most common treatment.

AIRBORNE ALLERGIES
An interesting allergy is pollen allergy. Humans have hay fever, rose fever and other fevers with which they suffer during the pollinating season. Many dogs suffer the same allergies. When the pollen count is high, your dog might suffer but don't expect him to sneeze and have a runny nose like humans. Dogs react to pollen allergies the same way they react

to fleas—they scratch and bite themselves.

Dogs, like humans, can be tested for allergens. Discuss the testing with your veterinary dermatologist.

FOOD PROBLEMS

FOOD ALLERGIES
Dogs are allergic to many foods that are best-sellers and highly recommended by breeders and veterinary surgeons. Changing the brand of food that you buy may not eliminate the problem if the element to which the dog is allergic is contained in the new brand.

Recognising a food allergy is difficult. Humans vomit or have rashes when they eat a food to which they are allergic. Dogs neither vomit nor (usually) develop a rash. They react in the same manner as they do to an airborne or flea allergy: they itch, scratch and bite, thus making the diagnosis extremely difficult. Whilst pollen allergies and parasite bites are usually seasonal, food allergies are year-round problems.

FOOD INTOLERANCE
Food intolerance is the inability of the dog to completely digest certain foods. Puppies that may have done very well on their mother's milk may not do well on cow's milk. The result of this food intolerance may be loose bowels,

108

passing gas and stomach pains. These are the only obvious symptoms of food intolerance, which makes diagnosis difficult.

TREATING FOOD PROBLEMS

It is possible to handle food allergies and food intolerance yourself. Put your dog on a diet that it has never had. Obviously if it has never eaten this new food it can't have been allergic or intolerant of it. Start with a single ingredient that is not in the dog's diet at the present time. Ingredients like chopped beef or fish are common in dog's diets, so try something more exotic like rabbit, pheasant or even just vegetables. Keep the dog on this diet (with no additives) for a month. If the symptoms of food allergy or intolerance disappear, chances are your dog has a food allergy.

Don't think that the single ingredient cured the problem. You still must find a suitable diet and ascertain which ingredient in the old diet was objectionable. This is most easily done by adding ingredients to the new diet one at a time. Let the dog stay on the modified diet for a month before you add another ingredient. Eventually, you will determine the ingredient that caused the adverse reaction.

An alternative method is to carefully study the ingredients in the diet to which your dog is allergic or intolerant. Identify the main ingredient in this diet and eliminate the main ingredient by buying a different food that does not have that ingredient. Keep experimenting until the symptoms disappear after one month on the new diet.

Many Weimaraners are allergic to the pollen in the air, especially during spring flowering time. If your dog scratches itself during specific times of the year, you should suspect an airborne or grass allergy.

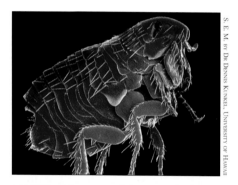

A scanning electron micrograph (S. E. M.) of a dog flea, *Ctenocephalides canis*.

S. E. M. by Dr Dennis Kunkel, University of Hawaii

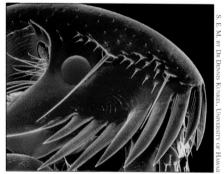

Magnified head of a dog flea, *Ctenocephalides canis*.

S. E. M. by Dr Dennis Kunkel, University of Hawaii

A male dog flea, *Ctenocephalides canis*.

EXTERNAL PARASITES

Of all the problems to which dogs are prone, none is more well known and frustrating than fleas. Flea infestation is relatively simple to cure but difficult to prevent. Parasites that are harboured inside the body are a bit more difficult to eradicate but they are easier to control.

FLEAS

To control a flea infestation you have to understand the flea's life cycle. Fleas are often thought of as a summertime problem but centrally heated homes have changed the patterns and fleas can be found at any time of the year. The most effective method of flea control is a two-stage approach:

Photo by Jean Claude Revy/Phototake.

one stage to kill the adult fleas, and the other to control the development of pre-adult fleas. Unfortunately, no single active ingredient is effective against all stages of the life cycle.

LIFE CYCLE STAGES
During its life, a flea will pass through four life stages: egg, larva, pupa and adult. The adult stage is the most visible and irritating stage of the flea life cycle and this is why the majority of flea-control products concentrate on this stage. The fact is that adult fleas account for only 1% of the total flea population, and the other 99% exist in pre-adult stages, i.e. eggs, larvae and pupae. The pre-adult stages are barely visible to the naked eye.

THE LIFE CYCLE OF THE FLEA
Eggs are laid on the dog, usually in quantities of about 20 or 30, several times a day. The female adult flea must have a blood meal

before each egg-laying session. When first laid, the eggs will cling to the dog's fur, as the eggs are still moist. However, they will quickly dry out and fall from the dog, especially if the dog moves around or scratches. Many eggs will fall off in the dog's favourite area or an area in which he spends a lot of time, such as his bed.

Once the eggs fall from the dog onto the carpet or furniture, they will hatch into larvae. This takes from one to ten days. Larvae are not particularly mobile, and will usually travel only a few inches from where they hatch. However, they do have a tendency to move

ILLUSTRATION COURTESY OF BAYER VITAL GMBH & CO. KG

A Look at Fleas

Fleas have been around for millions of years and have adapted to changing host animals. They are able to go through a complete life cycle in less than one month or they can extend their lives to almost two years by remaining as pupae or cocoons. They do not need blood or any other food for up to 20 months.

They have been measured as being able to jump 300,000 times and can jump 150 times their length in any direction including straight up. Those are just a few of the reasons why they are so successful in infesting a dog!

away from light and heavy traffic—under furniture and behind doors are common places to find high quantities of flea larvae.

The flea larvae feed on dead organic matter, including adult flea faeces, until they are ready to change into adult fleas. Fleas will usually remain as larvae for around seven days. After this period, the larvae will pupate into protective pupae. While inside the pupae, the larvae will undergo metamorphosis and change into adult fleas. This can take as little time as a few days, but the adult fleas can remain inside the pupae waiting to hatch for up to two years. The pupae are signalled to hatch by certain stimuli, such as physical pressure—the pupae's being stepped on, heat from an animal lying on the pupae or increased carbon dioxide levels and vibrations—indicating that a suitable host is available.

Once hatched, the adult flea must feed within a few days. Once the adult flea finds a host, it will not leave voluntarily. It only becomes dislodged by grooming or

EN GARDE: CATCHING FLEAS OFF GUARD

Consider the following ways to arm yourself against fleas:
• Add a small amount of pennyroyal or eucalyptus oil to your dog's bath. These natural remedies repel fleas.
• Supplement your dog's food with fresh garlic (minced or grated) and a hearty amount of brewer's yeast, both of which ward off fleas.
• Use a flea comb on your dog daily. Submerge fleas in a cup of bleach to kill them quickly.
• Confine the dog to only a few rooms to limit the spread of fleas in the home.
• Vacuum daily . . . and get all of the crevices! Dispose of the bag every few days until the problem is under control.
• Wash your dog's bedding daily. Cover cushions where your dog sleeps with towels, and wash the towels often.

DID YOU KNOW?

Never mix flea control products without first consulting your veterinary surgeon. Some products can become toxic when combined with others and can cause serious or fatal consequences.

the host animal's scratching. The adult flea will remain on the host for the duration of its life unless forcibly removed.

TREATING THE ENVIRONMENT AND THE DOG

Treating fleas should be a two-pronged attack. First, the environment needs to be treated; this includes carpets and furniture, especially the dog's bedding and

Opposite page: A scanning electron micrograph of a dog or cat flea, *Ctenocephalides*, magnified more than 100x. This image has been colourized for effect.

The Life Cycle of the Flea

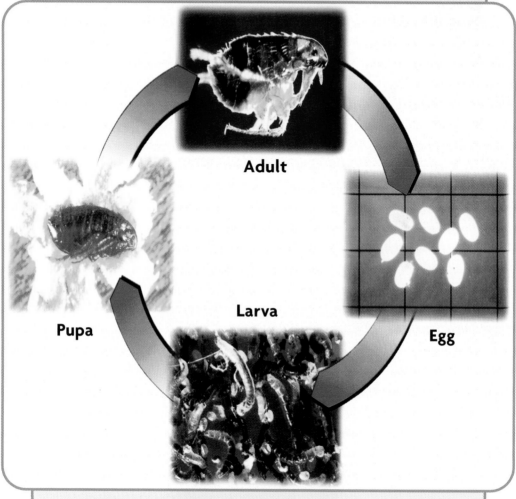

Adult

Pupa

Larva

Egg

This graphic depiction of the life cycle of the flea appears courtesy of Fleabusters®, R_x for fleas.

areas underneath furniture. The environment should be treated with a household spray containing an Insect Growth Regulator (IGR) and an insecticide to kill the adult fleas. Most IGRs are effective against eggs and larvae; they actually mimic the fleas' own hormones and stop the eggs and larvae from developing into adult fleas. There are currently no treatments available to attack the pupa stage of the life cycle, so the adult insecticide is used to kill the newly hatched adult fleas before

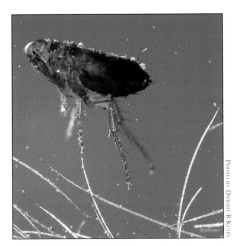

Photo by Dwight R Kuhn

Dwight R Kuhn's magnificent action photo showing a flea jumping from a dog's back.

TICKS AND MITES

Though not as common as fleas, ticks and mites are found all over the tropical and temperate world. They don't bite, like fleas; they harpoon. They dig their sharp proboscis (nose) into the dog's skin and drink the blood. Their only food and drink is dog's blood. Dogs can get Lyme disease, Rocky Mountain spotted fever (normally

they find a host. Most IGRs are active for many months, whilst adult insecticides are only active for a few days.

When treating with a household spray, it is a good idea to vacuum before applying the product. This stimulates as many pupae as possible to hatch into adult fleas. The vacuum cleaner should also be treated with a flea treatment to prevent the eggs and larvae that have been hoovered into the vacuum bag from hatching.

The second stage of treatment is to apply an adult insecticide to the dog. Traditionally, this would be in the form of a collar or a spray, but more recent innovations include digestible insecticides that poison the fleas when they ingest the dog's blood. Alternatively, there are drops that, when placed on the back of the animal's neck, spread throughout the fur and skin to kill adult fleas.

FLEA CONTROL

Two types of products should be used when treating fleas—a product to treat the pet and a product to treat the home. Adult fleas represent less than 1% of the flea population. The pre-adult fleas (eggs, larvae and pupae) represent more than 99% of the flea population and are found in the environment; it is in the case of pre-adult fleas that products containing an Insect Growth Regulator (IGR) should be used in the home.

IGRs are a new class of compounds used to prevent the development of insects. They do not kill the insect outright, but instead use the insect's biology against it to stop it from completing its growth. Products that contain methoprene are the world's first and leading IGRs. Used to control fleas and other insects, this type of IGR will stop flea larvae from developing and protect the house for up to seven months.

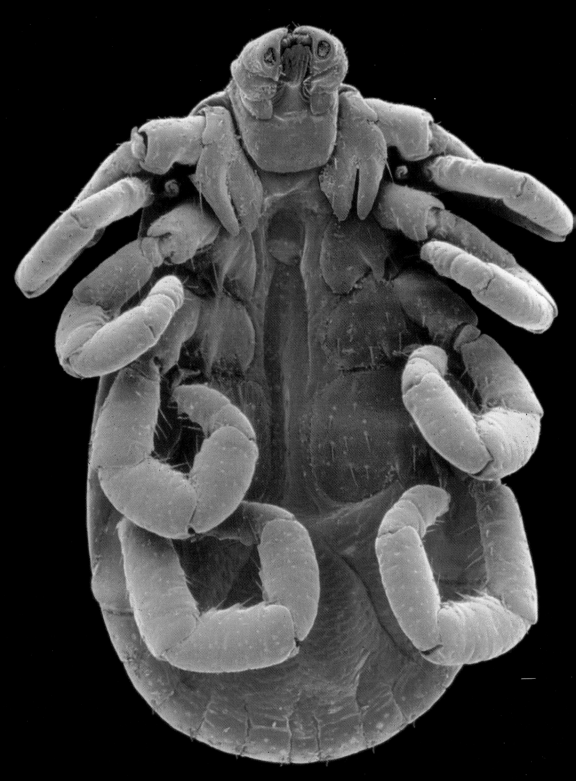

found in the US only), paralysis and many other diseases from ticks and mites. They may live where fleas are found and they like to hide in cracks or seams in walls wherever dogs live. They are controlled the same way fleas are controlled.

The dog tick, *Dermacentor variabilis*, may well be the most common dog tick in many geographical areas, especially those areas where the climate is hot and humid.

Most dog ticks have life expectancies of a week to six

ILLUSTRATION COURTESY OF BAYER VITAL GMBH & CO. KG

Beware the Deer Tick

The great outdoors may be fun for your dog, but it also is a home to dangerous ticks. Deer ticks carry a bacterium known as *Borrelia burgdorferi* and are most active in the autumn and spring. When infections are caught early, penicillin and tetracycline are effective antibiotics, but if left untreated the bacteria may cause neurological, kidney and cardiac problems as well as long-term trouble with walking and painful joints.

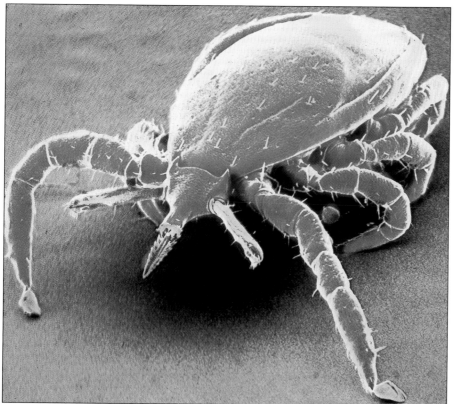

S. E. M. BY DR ANDREW SPIELMAN/PHOTOTAKE

A deer tick, the carrier of Lyme disease. This magnified micrograph has been colourized for effect.

Opposite page: The dog tick, *Dermacentor variabilis*, is probably the most common tick found on dogs. Look at the strength in its eight legs! No wonder it's hard to detach them.

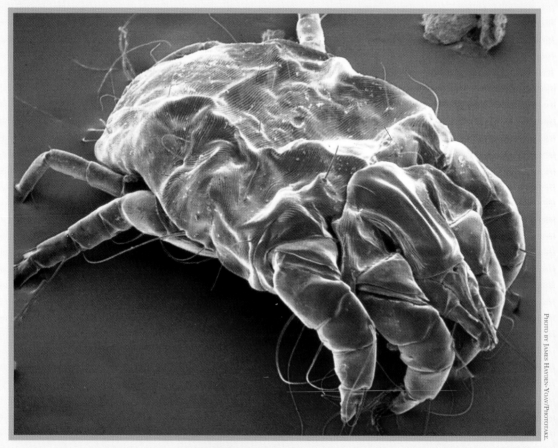

Photo by James Hayden-Yoav/Phototake.

Above:
The mange mite,
Psoroptes bovis.

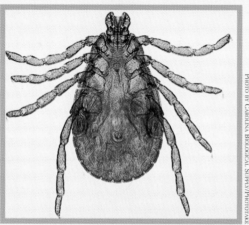

Photo by Carolina Biological Supply/Phototake

A brown dog tick, *Rhipicephalus sanguineus*, is
an uncommon but annoying tick found on dogs.

Photo by Dwight R Kuhn

Human lice look like dog lice;
the two are closely related

months, depending upon climatic conditions. They can neither jump nor fly, but they can crawl slowly and can range up to 5 metres (16 feet) to reach a sleeping or unsuspecting dog.

MANGE

Mites cause a skin irritation called mange. Some are contagious, like *Cheyletiella*, ear mites, scabies and chiggers. Mites that cause ear-mite infestations are usually controlled with Lindane, which can only be administered by a vet, followed by Tresaderm at home.

It is essential that your dog be treated for mange as quickly as possible because some forms of mange are transmissible to people.

INTERNAL PARASITES

Most animals—fishes, birds and mammals, including dogs and humans—have worms and other parasites that live inside their bodies. According to Dr Herbert R Axelrod, the fish pathologist, there are two kinds of parasites: dumb and smart. The smart parasites live in peaceful cooperation with their hosts (symbiosis), while the dumb parasites kill their host. Most of the worm infections are relatively easy to control. If they are not controlled they weaken the host dog to the point that other medical problems occur, but they are not dumb parasites.

ROUNDWORMS

The roundworms that infect dogs are scientifically known as *Toxocara canis*. They live in the dog's intestine. The worms shed eggs continually. It has been estimated that a dog produces about 150 grammes of faeces every day. Each gramme of faeces averages 10,000–12,000 eggs of roundworms. There are no known areas in which dogs roam that do not contain roundworm eggs. The greatest danger of roundworms is that they infect people too! It is

DEWORMING

Ridding your puppy of worms is VERY IMPORTANT because certain worms that puppies carry, such as tapeworms and roundworms, can infect humans.

Breeders initiate a deworming programme at or about four weeks of age. The routine is repeated every two or three weeks until the puppy is three months old. The breeder from whom you obtained your puppy should provide you with the complete details of the deworming programme.

Your veterinary surgeon can prescribe and monitor the programme of deworming for you. The usual programme is treating the puppy every 15–20 days until the puppy is positively worm free.

It is not advised that you treat your puppy with drugs that are not recommended professionally.

wise to have your dog tested regularly for roundworms.

Pigs also have roundworm infections that can be passed to humans and dogs. The typical roundworm parasite is called *Ascaris lumbricoides*.

HOOKWORMS

The worm *Ancylostoma caninum* is commonly called the dog hookworm. It is dangerous to humans and cats. It also has teeth by which it attaches itself to the intestines of the dog. It changes the site of its attachment about six times a day and the dog loses blood from each detachment, possibly causing iron-deficiency anaemia. Hookworms are easily purged from the dog with many medications. Milbemycin oxime,

ROUNDWORM

Average size dogs can pass 1,360,000 roundworm eggs every day.

For example, if there were only 1 million dogs in the world, the world would be saturated with 1,300 metric tonnes of dog faeces.

These faeces would contain 15,000,000,000 roundworm eggs.

It's known that 7–31% of home gardens and children's play boxes in the US contain roundworm eggs.

Flushing dog's faeces down the toilet is not a safe practice because the usual sewage treatments do not destroy roundworm eggs.

Infected puppies start shedding roundworm eggs at 3 weeks of age. They can be infected by their mother's milk.

The roundworm, *Rhabditis*. The roundworm can infect both dogs and humans.

PHOTO BY CAROLINA BIOLOGICAL SUPPLY/PHOTOTAKE

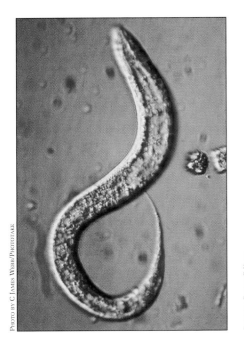

PHOTO BY C. JAMES WEBB/PHOTOTAKE

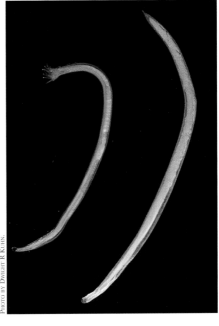

PHOTO BY DWIGHT R KUHN.

Left:
The infective stage of the hookworm larva.

Right:
Male and female hookworms, *Ancylostoma caninum*, are uncommonly found in pet or show dogs in Britain. Hookworms may infect other dogs that have exposure to grasslands.

which also serves as a heartworm preventative in Collies, can be used for this purpose.

In Britain the 'temperate climate' hookworm (*Uncinaria stenocephala*) is rarely found in pet or show dogs, but can occur in

DID YOU KNOW?

Never allow your dog to swim in polluted water or public areas where water quality can be suspect. Even perfectly clear water can harbour parasites, many of which can cause serious to fatal illnesses in canines. Areas inhabited by waterfowl and other wildlife are especially dangerous.

hunting packs, racing Greyhounds and sheepdogs because the worms can be prevalent wherever dogs are exercised regularly on grassland.

TAPEWORMS

There are many species of tapeworms. They are carried by fleas! The dog eats the flea and starts the tapeworm cycle. Humans can also be infected with tapeworms, so don't eat fleas! Fleas are so small that your dog could pass them onto your hands, your plate or your food and thus make it possible for you to ingest a flea which is carrying tapeworm eggs.

While tapeworm infection is not life threatening in dogs (smart parasite!), it can be the cause of a

121

The head and rostellum (the round prominence on the scolex) of a tapeworm, which infects dogs and humans.

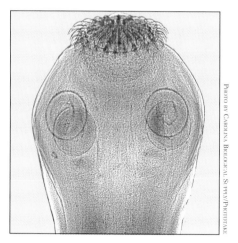

Photo by Carolina Biological Supply/Phototake

very serious liver disease for humans. About 50 percent of the humans infected with *Echinococcus multilocularis*, a type of tapeworm that causes alveolar hydatis, perish.

HEARTWORMS

Heartworms are thin, extended worms up to 30 cms (12 ins) long which live in a dog's heart and the major blood vessels surrounding it. Dogs may have up to 200 worms. Symptoms may be loss of energy, loss of appetite, coughing, the development of a pot belly and anaemia.

Heartworms are transmitted by mosquitoes. The mosquito drinks the blood of an infected dog and takes in larvae with the blood. The larvae, called microfilaria, develop within the body of the mosquito and are passed on to the next dog bitten after the larvae mature. It takes two to three weeks for the

TAPEWORM

Humans, rats, squirrels, foxes, coyotes, wolves, mixed breeds of dogs and purebred dogs are all susceptible to tapeworm infection. Except in humans, tapeworms are usually not a fatal infection.

Infected individuals can harbour a thousand parasitic worms.

Tapeworms have two sexes—male and female (many other worms have only one sex—male and female in the same worm).

If dogs eat infected rats or mice, they get the tapeworm disease.

One month after attaching to a dog's intestine, the worm starts shedding eggs. These eggs are infective immediately.

Infective eggs can live for a few months without a host animal.

Roundworms, whipworms and hookworms are just a few of the other commonly known worms that infect dogs.

larvae to develop to the infective stage within the body of the mosquito. Dogs should be treated at about six weeks of age, and maintained on a prophylactic dose given monthly.

Blood testing for heartworms is not necessarily indicative of how seriously your dog is infected. This is a dangerous disease. Although heartworm is a problem for dogs in America, Australia, Asia and Central Europe, dogs in the United Kingdom are not currently affected by heartworm.

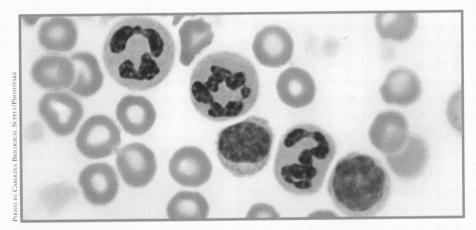

Magnified heartworm larvae, *Dirofilaria immitis*.

PHOTO BY CAROLINA BIOLOGICAL SUPPLY/PHOTOTAKE

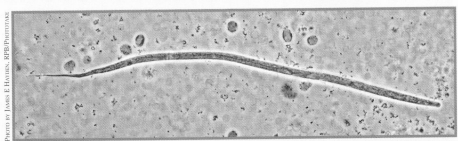

The heartworm, *Dirofilaria immitis*.

PHOTO BY JAMES E HAYDEN, RPB/PHOTOTAKE

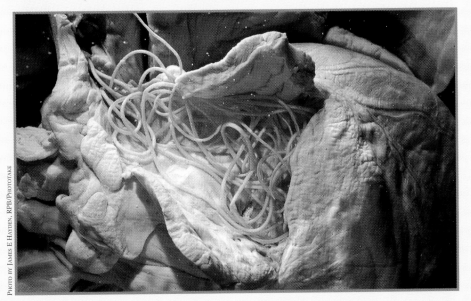

The heart of a dog infected with canine heartworm, *Dirofilaria immitis*.

PHOTO BY JAMES E HAYDEN, RPB/PHOTOTAKE

Owners and breeders are looking for Weimaraners with clear, healthy eyes.

A PET OWNER'S GUIDE TO COMMON OPHTHALMIC DISEASES
by Prof. Dr Robert L Peiffer, Jr.

Few would argue that vision is the most important of the cognitive senses, and maintenance of a normal visual system is important for an optimal quality of life. Likewise, pet owners tend to be acutely aware of their pet's eyes and vision, which is important because early detection of ocular disease will optimize therapeutic outcomes. The eye is a sensitive organ with minimal reparative capabilities, and with some diseases, such as glaucoma, uveitis and retinal detachment, delay in diagnosis and treatment can be critical in terms of whether vision can be preserved.

Lower entropion, or rolling in of the eyelid, is causing irritation in the left eye of this young dog. Several extra eyelashes, or distichiasis, are present on the upper lid.

The causes of ocular disease are quite varied; the nature of dogs make them susceptible to traumatic conditions, the most common of which include proptosis of the globe, cat scratch injuries and penetrating wounds from foreign objects, including sticks and air rifle pellets. Infectious diseases caused by bacteria, viruses or fungi may be localized to the eye or part of a systemic infection. Many of the common conditions, including eyelid conformational problems, cataracts, glaucoma and retinal degenerations have a genetic basis.

Before acquiring your puppy it is important to ascertain that both parents have been examined and certified free of eye disease by a veterinary ophthalmologist. Since many of these genetic diseases can be detected early in life, acquire the pup with the condition that it pass a thorough ophthalmic examination by a qualified specialist.

LID CONFORMATIONAL ABNORMALITIES
Rolling in (entropion) or out (ectropion) of the lids tends to be a breed-related problem. Entropion can involve the upper and/or lower lids. Signs usually appear between 3 and 12 months of age. The irritation caused by the eyelid hairs rubbing

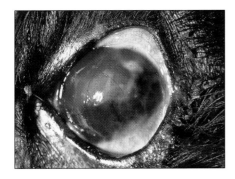

on the surface of the cornea may result in blinking, tearing and damage to the cornea. Ectropion is likewise breed-related and is considered 'normal' in hounds, for instance; unlike entropion, which results in acute discomfort, ectropion may cause chronic irritation related to exposure and the pooling of secretions. Most of these cases can be managed medically with daily irrigation with sterile saline and topical antibiotics when required.

EYELASH ABNORMALITIES
Dogs normally have lashes only on the upper lids, in contrast to humans. Occasionally, extra

eyelashes may be seen emerging at the eyelid margin (distichiasis) or through the inner surface of the eyelid (ectopic cilia).

CONJUNCTIVITIS
Inflammation of the conjunctiva, the pink tissue that lines the lids and the anterior portion of the sclera, is generally accompanied by redness, discharge and mild discomfort. The majority of cases are either associated with bacterial infections or dry eye syndrome. Fortunately, topical medications are generally effective in curing or controlling the problem.

DRY EYE SYNDROME
Dry eye syndrome (keratoconjunctivitis sicca) is a common cause of external ocular disease. Discharge is typically thick and sticky, and keratitis is a frequent component; any breed can be affected. While some cases can be associated with toxic effects of drugs, including the sulfa antibiotics, the cause in the majority of the cases cannot be determined and is assumed to be immune-mediated.

Keratoconjunctivitis sicca, seen here in the right eye of a middle-aged dog, causes a characteristic thick mucous discharge as well as secondary corneal changes.

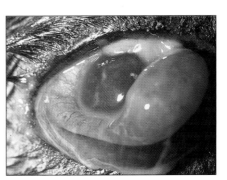

Left: Prolapse of the gland of the third eyelid in the right eye of a pup. Right: In this case, in the right eye of a young dog, the prolapsed gland can be seen emerging between the edge of the third eyelid and the corneal surface.

Multiple deep ulcerations affect the cornea of this middle-aged dog.

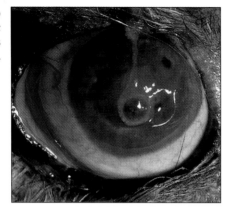

PROLAPSE OF THE GLAND OF THE THIRD EYELID

In this condition, commonly referred to as *cherry eye*, the gland of the third eyelid, which produces about one-third of the aqueous phase of the tear film and is normally situated within the anterior orbit, prolapses to emerge as a pink fleshy mass protruding over the edge of the third eyelid, between the third eyelid and the cornea. The condition usually develops during the first year of life and, while mild irritation may result, the condition is unsightly as much as anything else.

Lipid deposition can occur as a primary inherited dystrophy, or secondarily to hypercholesterolemia (in dogs frequently associated with hypothyroidism), chronic corneal inflammation or neoplasia. The deposits in this dog assume an oval pattern in the centre of the cornea.

CORNEAL DISEASE

The cornea is the clear front part of the eye that provides the first step in the collection of light on its journey to be eventually focused onto the retina, and most corneal diseases will be manifested by alterations in corneal transparency. The cornea is an exquisitely innervated tissue, and defects in corneal integrity are accompanied by pain, which is demonstrated by squinting.

Corneal ulcers may occur secondary to trauma or to irritation from entropion or ectopic cilia. In middle-aged or older dogs, epithelial ulcerations may occur spontaneously due to an inherent defect; these are referred to as indolent or Boxer ulcers, in recognition of the breed in which we see the condition most frequently. Infection may occur secondarily. Ulcers can be potentially blinding conditions; severity is dependent upon the size and depth of the ulcer and other complicating features.

Non-ulcerative keratitis tends to have an immune-mediated component and is managed by topical immunosuppressants, usually corticosteroids. Corneal edema can occur in elderly dogs. It is due to a failure of the corneal endothelial 'pump.'

The cornea responds to chronic irritation by transforming

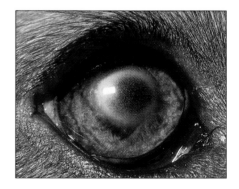

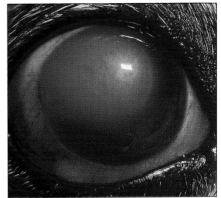

into skin-like tissue that is evident clinically by pigmentation, scarring and vascularization; some cases may respond to tear stimulants, lubricants and topical corticosteroids, while others benefit from surgical narrowing of the eyelid opening in order to enhance corneal protection.

UVEITIS

Inflammation of the vascular tissue of the eye–the uvea—is a common and potentially serious disease in dogs. While it may occur secondarily to trauma or other intraocular diseases, such as

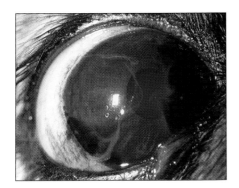

cataracts, most commonly uveitis is associated with some type of systemic infectious or neoplastic process. Uncontrolled, uveitis can lead to blinding cataracts, glaucoma and/or retinal detachments, and aggressive symptomatic therapy with dilating agents (to prevent pupillary adhesions) and anti-inflammatories are critical.

GLAUCOMA

The eye is essentially a hollow fluid-filled sphere, and the pressure within is maintained by regulation of the rate of fluid production and fluid egress at 10–20 mms of mercury. The retinal cells are extremely sensitive to elevations of intraocular pressure and, unless controlled, permanent blindness can occur within hours to days. In acute glaucoma, the conjunctiva becomes congested, the cornea cloudy, the pupil moderate and fixed; the eye is generally painful and avisual. Increased constant signs of

Corneal edema can develop as a slowly progressive process in elderly Boston Terriers, Miniature Dachshunds and Miniature Poodles, as well as others, as a result of the inability of the corneal endothelial 'pump' to maintain a state of dehydration.

Medial pigmentary keratitis in this dog is associated with irritation from prominent facial folds.

127

Weimaraner

Glaucoma in the dog most commonly occurs as a sudden extreme elevation of intraocular pressure, frequently to three to four times the norm. The eye of this dog demonstrates the common signs of episcleral injection, or redness; mild diffuse corneal cloudiness, due to edema; and a mid-sized fixed pupil.

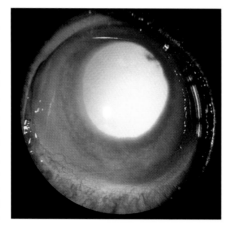

discomfort will accompany chronic cases.

Management of glaucoma is one of the most challenging situations the veterinary ophthalmologist faces; in spite of intense efforts, many of these cases will result in blindness.

CATARACTS AND LENS DISLOCATION
Cataracts are the most common blinding condition in dogs; fortunately, they are readily amenable to surgical intervention, with excellent results in terms of restoration of vision and replace-

ment of the cataractous lens with a synthetic one. Most cataracts in dogs are inherited; less commonly cataracts can be secondary to trauma, other ocular diseases, including uveitis, glaucoma, lens luxation and retinal degeneration, or secondary to an underlying systemic metabolic disease, including diabetes and Cushing's disease. Signs include a progressive loss of the bright dark appearance of the pupil, which is replaced by a blue-grey hazy appearance. In this respect, cataracts need to be distinguished from the normal ageing process of nuclear sclerosis, which occurs in middle-aged or older animals, and has minimal effect on vision.

Lens dislocation occurs in dogs and frequently leads to secondary glaucoma; early removal of the dislocated lens is generally curative.

RETINAL DISEASE
Retinal degenerations are usually inherited, but may be associated with vitamin E deficiency in dogs.

Left: The typical posterior subcapsular cataract appears between one and two years of age, but rarely progresses to where the animal has visual problems.
Right: Inherited cataracts generally appear between three and six years of age, and progress to the stage seen where functional vision is significantly impaired.

128

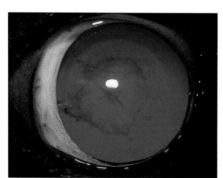

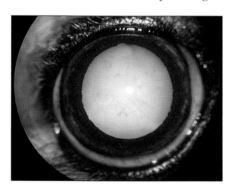

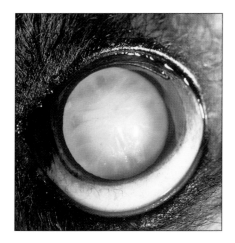

While signs are variable, most frequently one notes a decrease in vision over a period of months, which typically starts out as a night blindness. The cause of a more rapid loss of vision due to retinal degeneration occurs over days to weeks is labeled sudden acquired retinal degeneration or SARD; the outcome, however, is unfortunately usually similar to inherited and nutritional conditions, as the retinal tissues possess minimal regenerative capabilities. Most pets, however, with a bit of extra care and attention, show an amazing ability to adapt to an avisual world, and can be maintained as pets with a satisfactory quality of life. Detachment of the retina—due to accumulation of blood between the retina and the underling uvea, which is called the *choroid*—can occur secondarily to retinal tears or holes, tractional forces within the eye, or as a result of uveitis. These types of detachments may be amenable to surgical repair if diagnosed early.

OPTIC NERVE

Optic neuritis, or inflammation of the nerve that connects the eye with the brain stem, is a relatively uncommon condition that presents usually with rather sudden loss of vision and widely dilated non-responsive pupils.

Anterior lens luxation can occur as a primary disease in the terrier breeds, or secondarily to trauma. The fibres that hold the lens in place rupture and the lens may migrate through the pupil to be situated in front of the iris. Secondary glaucoma is a frequent and significant complication that can be avoided if the dislocated lens is removed surgically.

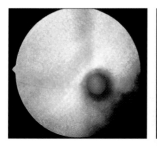
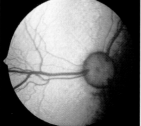
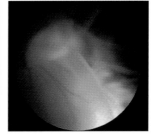

Left: The posterior pole of a normal fundus is shown; prominent are the head of the optic nerve and the retinal blood vessels. The retina is transparent, and the prominent green tapetum is seen superiorly.
Centre: An eye with inherited retinal dysplasia is depicted. The tapetal retina superior to the optic disc is disorganised, with multifocal areas of hyperplasia of the retinal pigment epithelium.
Right: Severe collie eye anomaly and a retinal detachment; this eye is unfortunately blind.

HOMEOPATHY:
an alternative to conventional medicine

'Less is Most'

Using this principle, the strength of a homeopathic remedy is measured by the number of serial dilutions that were undertaken to create it. The greater the number of serial dilutions, the greater the strength of the homeopathic remedy. The potency of a remedy that has been made by making a dilution of 1 part in 100 parts (or 1/100) is 1c or 1cH. If this remedy is subjected to a series of further dilutions, each one being 1/100, a more dilute and stronger remedy is produced. If the remedy is diluted in this way six times, it is called 6c or 6cH. A dilution of 6c is 1 part in 1000,000,000,000. In general, higher potencies in more frequent doses are better for acute symptoms and lower potencies in more infrequent doses are more useful for chronic, long-standing problems.

CURING OUR DOGS NATURALLY

Holistic medicine means treating the whole animal as a unique, perfect living being. Generally, holistic treatments do not suppress the symptoms that the body naturally produces, as do most medications prescribed by conventional doctors and vets. Holistic methods seek to cure disease by regaining balance and harmony in the patient's environment. Some of these methods include use of nutritional therapy, herbs, flower essences, aromatherapy, acupuncture, massage, chiropractic and, of course, the most popular holistic approach, homeopathy. Homeopathy is a theory or system of treating illness with small doses of substances which, if administered in larger quantities, would produce the symptoms that the patient already has. This approach is often described as 'like cures like.' Although modern veterinary medicine is geared toward the 'quick fix,' homeopathy relies on the belief that, given the time, the body is able to heal itself and return to its natural, healthy state.

Choosing a remedy to cure a problem in our dogs is the difficult part of homeopathy. Consult with your veterinary surgeon for a professional diagnosis of your dog's symptoms. Often these symptoms require immediate conventional care. If

your vet is willing, and somewhat knowledgeable, you may attempt a homeopathic remedy. Be aware that cortisone prevents homeopathic remedies from working. There are hundreds of possibilities and combinations to cure many problems in dogs, from basic physical problems such as excessive moulting, fleas or other parasites, unattractive doggy odour, bad breath, upset tummy, dry, oily or dull coat, diarrhoea, ear problems or eye discharge (including tears and dry or mucousy matter), to behavioural abnormalities, such as fear of loud noises, habitual licking, poor appetite, excessive barking, obesity and various phobias. From alumina to zincum metallicum, the remedies span the planet and the imagination…from flowers and weeds to chemicals, insect droppings, diesel smoke and volcanic ash.

Using 'Like to Treat Like'

Unlike conventional medicines that suppress symptoms, homeopathic remedies treat illnesses with small doses of substances that, if administered in larger quantities, would produce the symptoms that the patient already has. Whilst the same homeopathic remedy can be used to treat different symptoms in different dogs, here are some interesting remedies and their uses.

Apis Mellifica
(made from honey bee venom) can be used for allergies or to reduce swelling that occurs in acutely infected kidneys.

Diesel Smoke
can be used to help control travel sickness.

Calcarea Fluorica
(made from calcium fluoride which helps harden bone structure) can be useful in treating hard lumps in tissues.

Natrum Muriaticum
(made from common salt, sodium chloride) is useful in treating thin, thirsty dogs.

Nitricum Acidum
(made from nitric acid) is used for symptoms you would expect to see from contact with acids such as lesions, especially where the skin joins the linings of body orifices or openings such as the lips and nostrils.

Symphytum
(made from the herb knitbone, Symphytum officianale) is used to encourage bones to heal.

Urtica Urens
(made from the common stinging nettle) is used in treating painful, irritating rashes.

The term *old* is a qualitative term. For dogs, as well as their masters, old is relative. Certainly we can all distinguish between a puppy Weimaraner and an adult Weimaraner—there are the obvious physical traits, such as size, appearance and facial expressions, and personality traits. Puppies that are nasty are very rare. Puppies and young dogs like to play with children. Children's natural exuberance is a good match for the seemingly endless energy of young dogs. They like to run, jump, chase and retrieve. When dogs grow up and cease their interaction with children, they are often thought of as being too old to play with the kids.

On the other hand, if a Weimaraner is only exposed to people over 60 years of age, its life will normally be less active and it will not seem to be getting old as its activity level slows down.

If people live to be 100 years old, dogs live to be 20 years old. Whilst this is a good rule of thumb, it is very inaccurate. When trying to compare dog years to human years, you cannot make

From puppyhood to the senior years, your Weimaraner deserves quality care. With the 'grey ghost,' greying can be a bit deceptive, but white hairs on the muzzle are still detectable.

a generalisation about all dogs. You can make the generalisation that, 12 or 13 years is a good life span for a Weimaraner, which is quite good compared to many other purebred dogs that may only live to 8 or 9 years of age. Some Weimaraners have been known to live to 15 years. Dogs are generally considered mature within three years, but they can reproduce even earlier. So the first three years of a dog's life are like seven times that of comparable humans. That means a 3-year-old dog is like a 21-year-old human. As the curve of comparison shows, there is no hard and fast rule for comparing dog and human ages. The comparison is made even more difficult, for not all humans age at the same rate...and human females live longer than human males.

WHAT TO LOOK FOR IN SENIORS

Most veterinary surgeons and behaviourists use the seventh year mark as the time to consider a dog a 'senior.' The term 'senior' does not imply that the dog is geriatric and has begun to fail in mind and body. Ageing is essentially a slowing process. Humans readily admit that they feel a difference in their activity level from age 20 to 30, and then from 30 to 40, etc. By treating the seven-year-old dog as a senior, owners are able to implement certain therapeutic

Information . . .

You are your dog's caretaker and his dentist. Vets warn that plaque and tartar buildup on the teeth will damage the gums and allow bacteria to enter

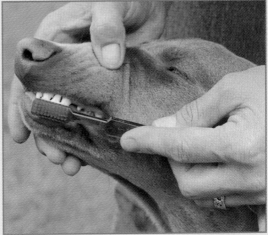

the dog's bloodstream, causing serious damage to the animal's vital organs. Studies show that over 50 percent of dogs have some form of gum disease before age three. Daily or weekly tooth cleaning (with a brush or soft gauze pad wipes) can add years to your dog's life.

and preventive medical strategies with the help of their veterinary surgeons. A senior-care programme should include at least two veterinary visits per year, screening sessions to determine the dog's health status, as well as nutritional counselling. Veterinary surgeons determine the senior dog's health status through a blood smear for a complete blood count, serum chemistry profile with electrolytes, urinalysis, blood pressure check, electrocardiogram, ocular tonometry (pressure on the eyeball) and dental prophylaxis.

Such an extensive programme for senior dogs is well advised before owners start to see the obvious physical signs of ageing, such as slower and inhibited movement, greying, increased sleep/nap periods and disinterest in play and other activity. This preventative programme promises a longer, healthier life for the ageing dog. Amongst the physical problems common in ageing dogs are the loss of sight and hearing,

arthritis, kidney and liver failure, diabetes mellitus, heart disease and Cushing's disease (a hormonal disease).

In addition to the physical manifestations discussed, there are some behavioural changes and problems related to ageing dogs. Dogs suffering from hearing or vision loss, dental discomfort or arthritis can become aggressive. Likewise the near-deaf and/or blind dog may be startled more easily and react in an unexpectedly aggressive manner. Seniors suffering from senility can become more impatient and irritable. Housesoiling accidents are associ-

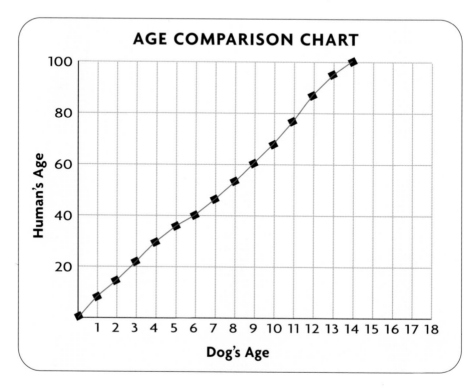

When Your Dog Gets Old...
Signs the Owner Can Look For

IF YOU NOTICE...	IT COULD INDICATE...
Discoloration of teeth and gums, foul breath, loss of appetite	Abcesses, gum disease, mouth lesions
Lumps, bumps, cysts, warts, fatty tumours	Cancers, benign or malignant
Cloudiness of eyes, apparent loss of sight	Cataracts, lenticular sclerosis, PRA, retinal dysplasia, blindness
Flaky coat, alopaecia (hair loss)	Hormonal problems, hypothyroidism
Obesity, appetite loss, excessive weight gain	Various problems
Household accidents, increased urination	Diabetes, kidney or bladder disease
Increased thirst	Kidney disease, diabetes mellitus
Change in sleeping habits, coughing	Heart disease
Difficulty moving	Arthritis, degenerative joint disease, spondylosis (degenerative spine disease)

If you notice any of these signs, an appointment should be made immediately with a veterinary surgeon for a thorough evaluation.

DID YOU KNOW?
Your senior dog may lose interest in eating, not because he's less hungry but because his senses of smell and taste have diminished. The old chow simply does not smell as good as it once did. Additionally, older dogs use less energy and thereby can sustain themselves on less food.

135

ated with loss of mobility, kidney problems and loss of sphincter control as well as plaque accumulation, physiological brain changes and reactions to medications. Older dogs, just like young puppies, suffer from separation anxiety, which can lead to excessive barking, whining, housesoiling and destructive behaviour. Seniors may become fearful of everyday sounds, such as vacuum cleaners, heaters, thunder and passing traffic. Some dogs have difficulty sleeping, due to discomfort, the need for frequent toilet visits and the like.

Owners should avoid spoiling the older dog with too many fatty treats. Obesity is a common problem in older dogs and subtracts years from their lifespan. Keep the senior dog as trim as possible since excessive weight

Seniors never understand why their worlds are slowing down. Be patient and loving with your senior to ensure that his golden years are as pleasant as possible.

puts additional stress on the body's vital organs. Some breeders recommend supplementing the diet with foods high in fibre and lower in calories. Adding fresh vegetables and marrow broth to the senior's diet makes a tasty, low-calorie, low-fat supplement. Vets also offer specialty diets for senior dogs that are worth exploring.

Your dog, as he nears his twilight years, needs his owner's patience and good care more than ever. Never punish an older dog for an accident or abnormal behaviour. For all the years of love, protection and companion-ship that your dog has provided, he deserves special attention and courtesies. The older dog may need to relieve himself at 3 a.m. because he can no longer hold it for eight hours. Older dogs may not be able to remain crated for more than two or three hours. It may be time to give up a sofa or chair to your old friend. Although he may not seem as enthusiastic about your attention and petting, he does appreciate the considera-tions you offer as he gets older.

Your Weimaraner does not understand why his world is slowing down. Owners must make the transition into the golden years as pleasant and rewarding as possible.

WHAT TO DO WHEN THE TIME COMES
You are never fully prepared to make a rational decision about putting your dog to sleep. It is very obvious that you love your Weimaraner or you would not be reading this book. Putting a loved dog to sleep is extremely difficult. It is a decision that must be made with your veterinary surgeon. You are usually forced to make the decision when one of the life-threatening symptoms listed above becomes serious enough for you to seek medical (veterinary) help.

If the prognosis of the malady indicates the end is near and your beloved pet will only suffer more and experience no enjoyment for the balance of its life, then euthanasia is the right choice.

WHAT IS EUTHANASIA?
Euthanasia derives from the Greek meaning *good death*. In other words, it means the planned, painless killing of a dog suffering from a painful, incurable condition, or who is so aged that it cannot walk, see, eat or control its excretory functions.

Euthanasia is usually

GETTING OLD

The bottom line is simply that a dog is getting old when YOU think it is getting old because it slows down in its general activities, including walking, running, eating, jumping and retrieving. On the other hand, certain activities increase,

such as more sleeping, more barking and more repetition of habits like going to the door without being called when you put your coat on to leave or go outdoors.

accomplished by injection with an overdose of an anaesthesia or barbiturate. Aside from the prick of the needle, the experience is usually painless.

MAKING THE DECISION

The decision to euthanise your dog is never easy. The days during which the dog becomes ill and the end occurs can be unusually stressful for you. If this is your first experience with the death of a loved one, you may need the comfort dictated by your religious beliefs. If you are the head of the family and have children, you should have involved them in the decision of putting your Weimaraner to sleep. Usually your dog can be maintained on drugs for a few days in order to give you ample time to make a decision. During this time, talking with members of your family or even people who have lived through this same experience can ease the burden of your inevitable decision.

THE FINAL RESTING PLACE

Dogs can have some of the same privileges as humans. They can occasionally be buried in a pet cemetery which is generally expensive, or if they have died at home can buried in your garden in a place suitably marked with some stone or newly planted tree or bush. Alternatively, they can be cremated and the ashes returned to you, or some people prefer to leave their dogs at the surgery for the vet to dispose of.

All of these options should be discussed frankly and openly with your veterinary surgeon. Do not

EUTHANASIA

Euthanasia must be done by a licensed veterinary surgeon. There also may be societies for the prevention of cruelty to animals in your area. They often offer this service upon a vet's recommendation.

Many pet cemeteries have facilities for storing a dog's ashes.

be afraid to ask financial questions. Cremations can be individual, but a less expensive option is mass cremation, although of course the ashes can not then be returned. Vets can usually arrange cremation services on your behalf, but you must be aware that in Britain if your dog has died at the surgery the vet cannot legally allow you to take your dog's body home.

GETTING ANOTHER DOG?

The grief of losing your beloved dog will be as lasting as the grief of losing a human friend or relative. In most cases, if your dog died of old age (if there is such a thing), it had slowed down considerably. Do you want a new Weimaraner puppy to replace it? Or are you better off in finding a more mature Weimaraner, say two to three years of age, which will usually be housetrained and will have an already developed personality. In this case, you can find out if you like each other after a few hours of being together.

The decision is, of course, your own. Do you want another Weimaraner or perhaps a different breed so as to avoid comparison with your beloved friend? Most people usually buy the same breed because they know (and love) the characteristics of that breed. Then, too, they often know people who have the same breed and perhaps they are lucky enough that a breeder they know and respect expects a litter soon. What could be better?

KEEPING SENIORS WARM

The coats of many older dogs become thinner as they age, which makes them more susceptible to cold and illness. During cold weather, limit time spent outdoors, and be extremely cautious with any artificial sources of warmth such as heat lamps, as these can cause severe burns. Your oldtimer may need a sweater to wear over his coat.

139

WEIMARANER

SHOW RING ETIQUETTE

Just as with anything else, there is a certain etiquette to the show ring that can only be learned through experience. Showing your dog can be quite intimidating to you as a novice when it seems as if everyone else knows what they are doing. You can familiarise yourself with ring procedure beforehand by taking a

class to prepare you and your dog for conformation showing or by talking with an experienced handler. When you are in the ring, listen and pay attention to the judge and follow his/her directions. Remember, even the most skilled handlers had to start somewhere. Keep it up and you too will become a proficient handler before too long!

When you purchased your Weimaraner, you should have made it clear to the breeder whether you wanted one just as a loveable companion and pet, or if you hoped to be buying a Weimaraner with show prospects. No reputable breeder will sell you a young puppy and tell you that it is definitely of show quality, for so much can go wrong during the early weeks and months of a puppy's development. If you plan to show, what you will hopefully have acquired is a puppy with 'show potential.'

To the novice, exhibiting a Weimaraner in the show ring may look easy but it takes a lot of hard work and devotion to win at a show such as the prestigious Crufts, not to mention a little luck too!

The first concept that the canine novice learns when watching a dog show is that each breed first competes against members of its own breed. Once the judge has selected the best member of each breed, provided that the show is judged on a Group system, that chosen dog will compete with other dogs in

its group. Finally, the best of each group will compete for Best in Show and Reserve Best in Show.

The second concept that you must understand is that the dogs are not actually compared against one another. The judge compares each dog against the breed standard, which is a written description of the ideal specimen of the breed. Whilst some early breed standards were indeed based on specific dogs that were famous or popular, many dedicated enthusiasts say that a perfect specimen, described in the standard, has never been bred. Thus the 'perfect' dog never walked into a show ring and, to the woe of dog breeders around the globe, does not exist. Breeders attempt to get as close to this ideal as possible with every litter, but theoretically the 'perfect' dog is so elusive that it is impossible (and if the 'perfect' dog were born, breeders and judges would never agree that it was indeed 'perfect').

141

How to Enter a Dog Show

1. Obtain an entry form and show schedule from the Show Secretary.
2. Select the classes that you want to enter and complete the entry form.

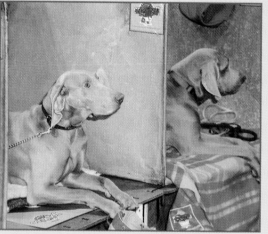

3. Transfer your dog into your name at The Kennel Club. (Be sure that this matter is handled before entering.)
4. Find out how far in advance show entries must be made. Oftentimes it's more than a couple of months.

If you are interested in exploring dog shows, your best bet is to join your local breed club. These clubs often host both Championship and Open Shows, and sometimes Match meetings and Special Events, all of which could be of interest, even if you are only an onlooker. Clubs also send out newsletters and some organise training days and seminars in order that people may learn more about their chosen breed. To locate the nearest breed club for you, contact The Kennel Club, the ruling body for the British dog world. The Kennel Club governs not only conformation shows but also working trials, obedience trials, agility trials and field trials. The Kennel Club furnishes the rules and regulations for all these events plus general dog registration and other basic requirements of dog ownership. Its annual show, called the Crufts Dog Show, held in Birmingham, is the largest benched show in England. Every year around 20,000 of the UK's best dogs qualify to participate in this marvellous show which lasts four days.

The Kennel Club governs many different kinds of shows in Great Britain, Australia, South Africa and beyond. At the most competitive and prestigious of these shows, the Championship Shows, a dog can earn Challenge Certificates, and thereby become a Show Champion or a Champion. To earn the prefix of 'Sh Ch' or 'Ch,' a dog must earn three Challenge Certificates under three different judges with at least one win occurring after the dog is one year old. CCs may be earned only at Championship Shows where a CC will be offered to each Best of Sex winner in their breed. Challenge Certificates are awarded to a very small percentage of the dogs competing, especially as dogs which are already Champions compete with others for these coveted CCs. The number of Challenge Certificates awarded in any one year is based upon the total number of dogs in each breed entered for competition.

There are three types of Championship Shows: an all-breed General Championship show for all Kennel-Club-recognised breeds; a Group Championship Show, limited to breeds within one of the groups; and a Breed Show, usually confined to a single breed. The Kennel Club determines which breeds at which Championship Shows will have the opportunity to earn Challenge Certificates (or 'tickets'). Serious exhibitors often will opt not to participate if the tickets are withheld at a particular show. This policy makes earning championships ever more difficult to accomplish.

Upon gaining three CCs in the show ring, the dog is designated a Show Champion (Sh Ch). In order to become a full Champion (Ch), Weimaraners and other Gundogs must first demonstrate their working ability in the field by earning a placement or a Certificate of Merit (CM) at a field trial, or by gaining a Show Gundog Working Certificate in a field test.

At a German dog show, all dogs are graded in categories of Excellent (VI), Very Good (SG), Good (G) and *Genugend*— Sufficient. The VI grade is extremely difficult to earn, and often only one is awarded during a single year. Additionally, a dog must earn four CCs to become a Show Champion in Germany, compared to three in the UK.

Open Shows are generally less competitive and are frequently

Classes at Dog Shows

There can be as many as 18 classes per sex for your breed. Check the show schedule carefully to make sure that you have entered your dog in the appropriate class. Among the classes offered can be:

Beginners; Minor Puppy (ages 6 to 9 months); Puppy (ages 6 to 12 months); Junior (ages 6 to 18 months); Beginners (handler or dog never won first place) as well as the following, each of which is defined in the schedule: Maiden; Novice; Tyro; Debutant; Undergraduate; Graduate; Postgraduate; Minor Limit; Mid Limit; Limit; Open; Veteran; Stud Dog; Brood Bitch; Progeny; Brace and Team.

At benched shows, areas like these are provided where the dogs wait until their turn in the ring.

used as 'practice shows' for young dogs. There are hundreds of Open Shows each year that can be delightful social events and are great first show experiences for the novice. Even if you're considering just watching a show to wet your paws, an Open Show is a great choice.

Whilst Championship and Open Shows are most important for the beginner to understand, there are other types of shows in which the interested dog owner can participate. Training clubs sponsor Matches that can be entered on the day of the show for

DID YOU KNOW?

The FCI *does not* issue pedigrees. The FCI members and contract partners are responsible for issuing pedigrees and training judges in their own countries. The FCI does maintain a list of judges and makes sure that they are recognised throughout the FCI member countries.

The FCI also *does not* act as a breeder referral; breeder information is available from FCI-recognised national canine societies in each of the FCI's member countries.

a nominal fee. In these introductory-level exhibitions, two dogs are pulled out of a hat and 'matched,' the winner of that match goes on to the next round and eventually only one dog is left undefeated.

Exemption Shows are much more light-hearted affairs with usually only four pedigree classes and several 'fun' classes, all of which can be entered on the day. Exemption Shows are sometimes held in conjunction with small agricultural shows and the proceeds must be given to a charity. A few Limited Shows are also available, but entry is restricted to members of the club

Performing before the judge so that he can appraise the Weimaraner's gait. Here is where HEEL training is so critical.

DID YOU KNOW?

You can get information about dog shows from kennel clubs and breed clubs:

Fédération Cynologique Internationale
14, rue Leopold II, B-6530 Thuin, Belgium
www.fci.be

The Kennel Club
1-5 Clarges St., Piccadilly, London W1Y 8AB, UK
www.the-kennel-club.org.uk

American Kennel Club
5580 Centerview Drive
Raleigh, NC 27606-3390, USA
www.akc.org

Canadian Kennel Club
89 Skyway Ave., Suite 100
Etobicoke, Ontario M9W 6R4 Canada
www.ckc.ca

that hosts the show, although one can usually join the club when making an entry.

Before you actually step into the ring, you would be well advised to sit back and observe the judge's ring procedure. If it is your first time in the ring, do not be over-anxious and run to the front of the line. It is much better to stand back and study how the exhibitor in front of you is performing. The judge asks each handler to 'stand' the dog, hopefully showing the dog off to his best advantage. The judge will observe the dog from a distance and from different angles, approach the dog, check his teeth, overall structure, alertness and muscle tone, as

The judge will closely evaluate the dog's structural conformation, including the bite, musculature and, for males, the presence of both testicles.

At Crufts, the UK's most prestigious dog show, there are hundreds of classes offered. Here the Weimaraner has been handled to Reserve Best in the Junior Handlers' competition. The young man with the Pointer won Best.

well as consider how well the dog 'conforms' to the standard. Most importantly, the judge will have the exhibitor move the dog around the ring in some pattern that he or she should specify (another advantage to not going first, but always listen since some judges change their directions—and the judge is always right!). Finally, the judge will give the dog one last look before moving on to the next exhibitor.

If you are not in the top three at your first show, do not be discouraged. Be patient and consistent and you may eventually find yourself in the winning lineup. Remember that the winners were once in your shoes and have devoted many hours and much money to earn the placement. If you find that your dog is losing every time and never getting a nod, it may be time to consider a different dog sport or just enjoy your Weimaraner as a pet.

DID YOU KNOW?

The Kennel Club divides its dogs into seven Groups: Gundogs, Utility, Working, Toy, Terrier, Hounds and Pastoral.*

*The Pastoral Group, established in 1999, includes those sheepdog breeds previously categorised in the Working Group.

The world's oldest dog show is the Westminster Kennel Club Dog Show, which takes place annually in New York City. The Group finals are completely televised, and the show has an attendance of more than 50,000 people per day.

WINNING THE TICKET

Earning a championship at Kennel Club shows is the most difficult in the world. Compared to the United States and Canada where it is relatively not 'challenging,' collecting

three green tickets not only requires much time and effort, it can be very expensive! Challenge Certificates, as the tickets are properly known, are the building blocks of champions— good breeding, good handling, good training and good luck!

WORKING TRIALS

Not to be confused with working tests, working trials are similar to obedience trials in the United States. Title categories are Companion Dog (CD), Utility Dog (UD), Working Dog (WD), Tracking Dog (TD) and Patrol Dog (PD). Weimaraners have enjoyed great success in UK working trials, with many earning titles up to the UD level. Training for these events is similar to that of field trial work, with more emphasis on obedience and control.

Working trials can be entered by any well-trained dog of any breed, not just Gundogs or Working dogs. Many dogs that earn the Kennel Club Good Citizen Dog award choose to participate in a working trial. As in conformation shows, dogs compete against a standard and if the dog reaches the qualifying mark, it obtains a certificate. Divided into groups, each exercise must be achieved 70 percent in order to qualify. If the dog achieves 80 percent in the open level, it receives a Certificate of Merit (COM); in the championship level, it receives a Qualifying Certificate.

At the CD stake, dogs must participate in four groups: Control, Stay, Agility and Search (Retrieve and Nosework). At the next three levels, UD, WD and TD, there are only three groups: Control, Agility and Nosework.

Agility consists of three jumps: a vertical scale up a wall of planks; a clear jump over a basic hurdle with a removable top bar; and a long jump across angled planks.

To earn the UD, WD and TD, dogs must track approximately one-half mile for articles laid from one-half hour to three hours ago. Tracks consist of turns and legs, and fresh ground is used for each participant.

The fifth stake, PD, involves teaching manwork, which is not recommended for every breed.

FIELD TRIALS AND WORKING TESTS

In the UK, working tests are licensed by The Kennel Club and generally held on private property with permission from the property's owner. Most tests offer three levels of difficulty: a Puppy Class (6–18 months), a Novice Class (for any dog not having won a Novice, Graduate or Open test) and the Open Class, which is open to all dogs regardless of previous experience or wins. While a Puppy Class may require simple obedience and a marked retrieve, an Open test might include hunting and

pointing out-of-sight caged game, a blind retrieve, possibly over water, and retrieves to test the steadiness of the dog.

Field trials are also licensed by The Kennel Club and are competitive events that evaluate the abilities of the dog. Separate categories of field trials are designed to test each Gundog group: Retrievers and Water Spaniels, Sporting Spaniels, Pointers and Setters, and Hunt, Point and Retrieve (HPR) breeds like the Weimaraner. All licensed field trials involve live game to be hunted, shot and retrieved.

As of 1996, only one Weimaraner had earned Field

DID YOU KNOW?

FCI-recognised breeds are divided into ten groups:
Group 1: Sheepdogs and Cattledogs (except Swiss Cattledogs)
Group 2: Pinschers and Schnauzers, Molossians, Swiss Mountain Dogs and Swiss Cattledogs
Group 3: Terriers
Group 4: Dachshunds
Group 5: Spitz- and primitive-type dogs
Group 6: Scenthounds and related breeds
Group 7: Pointing dogs
Group 8: Retrievers, Flushing dogs and Water dogs
Group 9: Companion and Toy dogs
Group 10: Sighthounds

A GENTLEMAN'S SPORT

Whether or not your dog wins top
honours, showing is a pleasant
social event. Sometimes, one may
meet a troublemaker or nasty
exhibitor, but these people should
be ignored and forgotten. In the
extremely rare case that someone
threatens or harasses you or your
dog, you can lodge a complaint
with The Kennel Club. This should
be done with extreme prudence.
Complaints are investigated
seriously and should never be filed
on a whim.

moderately popular amongst dog
folk. Whilst breeders of Working
and Gundog breeds concern
themselves with the field abilities
of their dogs, there is considerably
less interest in field trials than
dog shows.

AGILITY TRIALS

Agility trials began in the United
Kingdom in 1977 and have since
spread around the world,
especially to the United States,
where agility enjoys strong
popularity. The handler directs
his dog over an obstacle course
that includes jumps (such as
those used in the working trials),
as well as tyres, the dog walk,
weave poles, pipe tunnels,
collapsed tunnels, etc. The
Kennel Club requires that dogs
not be trained for agility until
they are 12 months old. This dog
sport intends to be great fun for
dog and owner and interested
owners should join a training
club that has obstacles and
experienced agility handlers who
can introduce you and your dog
to the 'ropes' (and tyres, tunnels
and so on).

FÉDÉRATION CYNOLOGIQUE INTERNATIONALE

Established in 1911, the Fédération Cynologique Internationale
(FCI) represents the 'world
kennel club.' This international
body brings uniformity to the
breeding, judging and showing of

Trial Champion status, Wobrooke
of Fleetapple owned by Di
Arrowsmith. In competition with
other HPR breeds, the ground-
scenting Weimaraner is naturally
slower and more methodical in
the hunt, and its independent
nature, which is a great asset in
rough shooting, puts it at a
disadvantage in competitive
situations requiring great control.

Working tests are frequently
used to prepare dogs for field
trials, the purpose of which is to
heighten the instincts and natural
abilities of Gundogs. Live game is
not used in working tests. Unlike
field trials, working tests do not
count toward a dog's record at
The Kennel Club, though the
same judges often oversee
working tests. Field trials began in
England in 1947 and are only

purebred dogs. Although the FCI originally included only four European nations, France, Holland, Austria and Belgium (which remains its headquarters), the organisation today embraces nations on six continents and recognises well over 300 breeds of purebred dog. There are three titles attainable through the FCI: the International Champion, which is the most prestigious; the International Beauty Champion, which is based on aptitude certificates in different countries; and the International Trial Champion, which is based on achievement in obedience trials in different countries. Quarantine laws in England and Australia prohibit most of their exhibitors from entering FCI shows. The rest of the Continent do participate in these impressive canine spectacles, the largest of which is the World Dog Show, hosted in a different country each year. FCI sponsors both national and international shows. The hosting country determines the judging system and breed standards are always based on the breed's country of origin.

Weimaraners are very agile and trainable dogs who frequently perform well in agility trials. This is Scooter, owned by Gayle Bock, clearly clearing the wall.

GLOSSARY

This glossary is intended to help you, the Weimaraner owner, better understand the specific terms used in this book as well as other terms that might surface in discussions with your veterinary surgeon during his care of your Weimaraner.

Abscess a pus-filled inflamed area of body tissue.

Acral lick granuloma unexplained licking of an area, usually the leg, that prevents healing of original wound.

Acute disease a disease whose onset is sudden and fast.

Albino an animal totally lacking in pigment (always white).

Allergy a known sensitivity that results from exposure to a given allergen.

Alopecia lack of hair.

Amaurosis an unexplained blindness from the retina.

Anaemia red-blood-cell deficiency.

Arthritis joint inflammation.

Atopic dermatitis congenital-allergen-caused inflammation of the skin.

Atrophy wasting away caused by faulty nutrition; a reduction in size.

Bloat gastric dilatation.

Calculi mineral 'stone' located in a vital organ, i.e. gall bladder.

Cancer a tumour that continues to expand and grow rapidly.

Carcinoma cancerous growth in the skin.

Cardiac arrhythmia irregular heartbeat.

Cardiomyopathy heart condition involving the septum and flow of blood.

Cartilage strong but pliable body tissue.

Cataract clouding of the eye lens.

Cherry eye third eyelid prolapsed gland.

Cleft palate improper growth of the two hard palates of the mouth.

Collie eye anomaly congenital defect of the back of the eye.

Congenital not the same as hereditary, but present at birth.

Congestive heart failure fluid buildup in lungs due to heart's inability to pump.

Conjunctivitis inflammation of the membrane that lines eyelids and eyeball.

Cow hocks poor rear legs that point inward; always incorrect.

Cryptorchid male animal with only one or both testicles undescended.

Cushing's disease condition caused by adrenal gland producing too much corticosteroid.

Cyst uninflamed swelling contain non-pus-like fluid.

Degeneration deterioration of tissue.

Demodectic mange red-mite infestation caused by *Demodex canis*.

Dermatitis skin inflammation.

Dew claw a functionless digit found on the inside of a dog's leg.

Diabetes insipidus disease of the hypothalamus gland resulting in animal passing great amounts of diluted urine.

Diabetes mellitus excess of glucose in blood stream.

Distemper contagious viral disease of dogs that can be most deadly.

Distichiasis double layer of eyelashes on an eyelid.

Dysplasia abnormal, poor development of a body part, especially a joint.

Dystrophy inherited degeneration.

Eclampsia potentially deadly disease in post-partum bitches due to calcium deficiency.

Ectropion outward turning of the eyelid; opposite of entropion.

Eczema inflammatory skin disease, marked by itching.

Edema fluid accumulation in a specific area.

Entropion inward turning of the eyelid.

Epilepsy chronic disease of the nervous system characterized by seizures.

Exocrine pancreatic insufficiency body's inability to produce enough enzymes to aid digestion.

False pregnancy pseudo-pregnancy, bitch shows all signs of pregnancy but there is no fertilization.

Follicular mange demodectic mange.

Gastric dilatation bloat caused by the dog's swallowing air resulting in distended, twisted stomach.

Gastroenteritis stomach or intestinal inflammation.

Gingivitis gum inflammation caused by plaque buildup.

Glaucoma increased eye pressure affecting vision.

Haematemesis vomiting blood.

Haematoma blood-filled swollen area.

Haematuria blood in urine.

Haemophilia bleeding disorder due to lack of clotting factor.

Haemorrhage bleeding.

Heat stroke condition due to over-heating of an animal.

Heritable an inherited condition.

Hot spot moist eczema characterised by dog's licking in same area.

Hyperglycemia excess glucose in blood.

Hypersensitivity allergy.

Hypertrophic cardiomyopathy left-ventricle septum becomes thickened and obstructs blood flow to heart.

Hypertrophic osteodystrophy condition affecting normal bone development.

Hypothyroidism disease caused by insufficient thyroid hormone.

Hypertrophy increased cell size resulting in enlargement of organ.

Hypoglycemia glucose deficiency in blood.

Idiopathic disease of unknown cause.

IgA deficiency immunoglobin deficiency resulting in digestive, breathing and skin problems.

Inbreeding mating two closely related animals, e.g., mother—son.

Inflammation the changes that occur to a tissue after injury, characterised by swelling, redness, pain, etc.

Jaundice yellow colouration of mucous membranes.

Keratoconjunctivitis sicca dry eye.

Leukaemia malignant disease charac-terised by white blood cells released into blood stream.

Lick granuloma excessive licking of a wound, preventing proper healing.

Merle coat colour that is diluted.

Monorchid a male animal with only one testicle descended.

Neuritis nerve inflammation.

Nicitating membrane third eyelid pulling across the eye.

Nodular dermatofibrosis lumps on toes and legs, usually associated with cancer of kidney and uterus.

Osteochondritis bone or cartilage inflammation.

Outcrossing mating two breed representatives from different families.

Pancreatitis pancreas inflammation.

Pannus chronic superficial keratitis, affecting pigment and blood vessels of cornea.

Panosteitis inflammation of leg bones, characterised by lameness.

Papilloma wart.

Patellar luxation slipped kneecap, common in small dogs.

Patent ductus arteriosus an open blood vessel between pulmonary artery and aorta.

Penetrance frequency in which a trait shows up in offspring of animals carrying that inheritable trait.

Periodontitis acute or chronic inflam-mation of tissue surrounding the tooth.

Pneumonia lung inflammation.

Progressive retinal atrophy congenital disease of retina causing blindness.

Pruritis persistent itching.

Retinal atrophy thin retina.

Seborrhea dry scurf or excess oil deposits on the skin.

Stomatitis mouth inflammation.

Tumour solid or fluid-filled swelling resulting from abnormal growth.

Uremia waste product buildup in blood due to disease of kidneys.

Uveitis inflammation of the iris.

Von Willebrand's disease hereditary bleeding disease.

Wall eye lack of colour in the iris.

Weaning separating the mother from her dependent, nursing young.

Zoonosis animal disease communicable to humans.

INDEX

*Page numbers in **boldface** indicate illustrations.*

𝕸𝖞 𝖂𝖊𝖎𝖒𝖆𝖗𝖆𝖓𝖊𝖗

PUT YOUR PUPPY'S FIRST PICTURE HERE

Dog's Name _____

Date _____ Photographer _____